52
OFFBEAT
TEXAS
STOPS

Published in 1993 by
Phillips Productions, Inc.
606 Young Street
Dallas, Texas 75202-4810

Printed in Hong Kong by Regent Publishing Services Limited
Second Printing, January 1994

Library of Congress Cataloging in Publication Data
52 Offbeat Texas Stops
Traveling with Bob Phillips, Texas Country Reporter
93-092751
ISBN 0-9636541-1-X

Designed by Jerry Price

52
OFFBEAT
TEXAS
STOPS

TRAVELING WITH
BOB PHILLIPS
TEXAS COUNTRY REPORTER

By Bob Phillips

606 Young Street
Dallas, TX 75202-4810

Contents

Stop #1   Ovilla Store, Ovilla .... pg. 11
Stop #2   Texas Exotic Feline Foundation, Boyd .... pg. 14
Stop #3   Snow Cone Man, Gainesville .... pg. 17
Stop #4   Pecan Art Museum, Denton .... pg. 19
Stop #5   Harvesters, Ennis .... pg. 22
Stop #6   Majestic Theatre, Wills Point .... pg. 25
Stop #7   Brewers Bell Museum, Canton .... pg. 27
Stop #8   Pine Mills Potters, Pine Mills .... pg. 29
Stop #9   Kitchen's Hardware, Mineola .... pg. 31
Stop #10   Edom Art Fair, Edom .... pg. 34
Stop #11   Whirlygig Man, Hawkins .... pg. 36
Stop #12   Ramage Farms, Hooks .... pg. 40
Stop #13   Milton Watts, Lake O' The Pines .... pg. 43
Stop #14   Historic Jefferson, Jefferson .... pg. 46
Stop #15   Mann Perry, Caddo Lake .... pg. 48
Stop #16   Jonesville Store, Jonesville .... pg. 50
Stop #17   Cane Syrup Makers, Troup .... pg. 53
Stop #18   Millard's Crossing, Nacogdoches .... pg. 56
Stop #19   The Old Time String Shop, Nacogdoches ...... pg. 59
Stop #20   Picture Collector, Wells .... pg. 61
Stop #21   Dinosaur Garden, Moscow .... pg. 64
Stop #22   Johnson Rock Shop, Livingston .... pg. 67
Stop #23   Timber Ridge Tours, Kountz .... pg. 70
Stop #24   Elissa, Galveston .... pg. 72
Stop #25   George Observatory, Needville .... pg. 74
Stop #26   Burton Cotton Gin, Burton .... pg. 76
Stop #27   Stuermer Store, Ledbetter .... pg. 79
Stop #28   Whoopers, Rockport .... pg. 82
Stop #29   Amazin' Walter, South Padre Island .... pg. 85
Stop #30   Gruene Honky-Tonk, Gruene .... pg. 88
Stop #31   Cave Without a Name, Boerne .... pg. 91
Stop #32   Old West Museum, Fredericksburg .... pg. 93
Stop #33   Westcave Preserve, Cypress Mill .... pg. 95
Stop #34   Vanishing Texas River Cruise, Burnet .... pg. 98
Stop #35   The Grove, The Grove .... pg. 101
Stop #36   Father Rosetti, Christoval .... pg. 103
Stop #37   Paint Rock Excursions, Paint Rock .... pg. 106
Stop #38   R.E. Donaho Concho Saddles, San Angelo ..... pg. 108
Stop #39   Third of July Celebration, San Angelo .... pg. 110
Stop #40   Opal Hunt's Living Museum, Bradshaw .... pg. 113
Stop #41   Dr. Pepper Plant, Dublin .... pg. 115
Stop #42   Hot Wells, South Bend .... pg. 118
Stop #43   Hotel Turkey, Turkey .... pg. 120
Stop #44   Barbed Wire & Route 66 Museum, McLean ..... pg. 123
Stop #45   Cowboy Morning Breakfast, Palo Duro Canyon .. pg. 126
Stop #46   Chevy Man, Lubbock .... pg. 127
Stop #47   Dean Leonard's Hat Shop, Lubbock .... pg. 130
Stop #48   God's Country, Crosbyton .... pg. 132
Stop #49   The Record Shop, Big Spring .... pg. 134
Stop #50   Marfa Lights, Marfa .... pg. 136
Stop #51   Rock Ranch, Alpine .... pg. 139
Stop #52   Redford Library, Redford .... pg. 141

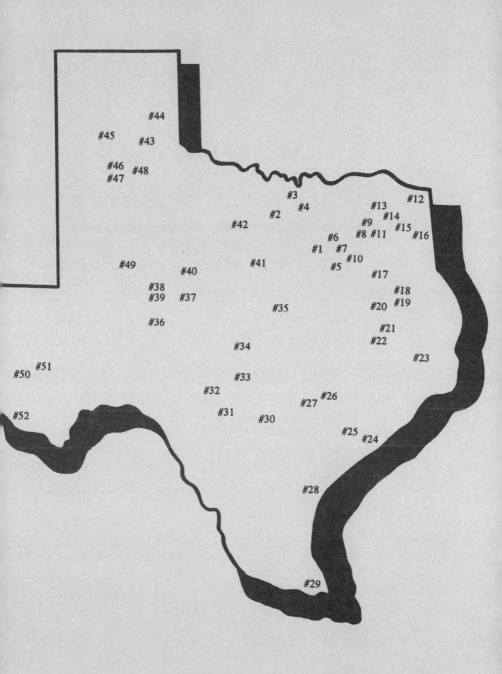

These are approximate locations of the 52 stops.

5

DEDICATION

To Papa, who taught me that everyone has a story
and
To Mama, who gave me the ambition to find out what it is.

ACKNOWLEDGMENTS

You will notice as you read this book that the word "we" is used far more often than the word "I". This is not the "royal we" used by kings and queens. It is the "collective we" used by a team that accomplishes something together. Long ago, I learned that the making of television is not a one person job. It's impossible. For every news anchor you see sitting at the desk, there are untold numbers of people who shoot the videotape, write the stories, set the lights and so on. And for every traveling television reporter you watch wandering the backroads, there are untold numbers of people who work hard to bring you those images. I'm sure it is much more romantic to imagine a lone explorer as he discovers new people and places, but it just ain't so. The same is true for creating a book. There are many people besides the writer who make it happen. Thanks to M'Layne Murphy for ramrodding the project. Otherwise, I would still be talking about writing it "someday". Thanks to Suzanne Stone for editing the words into logical paragraphs so other people can read them, too. Thanks to Jerry Price for the art direction and to Nancy Michalewicz for the cover photo, to Carl Walz, Inc., St. Louis, Missouri, for the creative cover photo frame, and to Milton Watts and Don Taylor for allowing us to include their poems. And thanks to all the folks at Phillips Productions for making these stories possible to tell in the first place and for taking up the slack I left the times I disappeared to write. And, of course, thanks to the viewers who keep watching so we can keep traveling.

Most of all, though, thanks to Jason Anderson, "Texas Country Reporter" producer, for sticking by me all these years and making this job fun and making this job make sense when it sometimes did not. Without Jason, this project could not and would not have happened. I am lucky to have such a great and loyal friend.

Crossing the much asked about Regency Bridge.

Preface

I never expected this job to last so long. When I started traveling the backroads in the early 70s, I always thought of it in terms of "a few more months". But the months turned into years and the years turned into decades and before long a score had passed. In the early years, I always expected someone to call me in off the road and tell me to do some "real" television stories, but now I kind of think it was easier to forget about me and where I was and what I was doing. So I kept sending back stories and gas receipts and, for whatever reason, folks kept watching. For that I am very grateful.

The idea was always to seek out the people you don't read about in the morning paper or see on the evening news and tell others about their lives. A few folks have asked over the years why I would want to do that and who cares about that anyway. The answer, apparently, is "lots of people care." I think that's part of life, to watch what's going on around us so we can have some basis for how we're doing, to know what others think and feel so we can judge our own lives against theirs. Otherwise, why would we watch the news? It's all part of the human experience.

Hardly a day goes by that we don't get letters and phone calls from folks who watch our television show wanting to know about places they can go. Most of them are looking for something a little unusual. They already know about the places we call the "chamber of commerce attractions", those Six Flags, Sea World, wax museum places that bring in lots of people and lots of money. "We want to know about some of the places you tell us about on television," most say. "Send me a list." When we tell them we don't keep such a list, they usually say something like "you oughta write a book." So we did.

We have tried to tell you about the unusual, the offbeat. Most of the places you will read about in the following pages are not destinations, they are stops, places worthy of a visit but not intended for a lengthy stay. With a few exceptions, most of the folks we tell you about are not set up to handle huge crowds of people. That's part of their charm, the fact that these are real people just doing what they do for themselves. Most are willing to let you stop by and watch them do it. By the way, the photos in the book were taken from the video shown on the television show.

Our suggestion is that you read through the book and throw it in your glove box along with "The Roads of Texas" atlas. Then, anytime you find yourself wandering the backroads, you can pull it out to find the places that aren't listed in the trip planner you got from the automobile club. I think you'll be glad you did.

Before we get started, we want to take a minute and answer two questions that we are asked several times a day. The first one is "What's the name of your "Texas Country Reporter" theme song, and how can I get a copy?" It's called "Hill Country Theme" and the version you hear at the beginning of the show is from an album by the Boston Pops titled "Pops Goes West". It's out of print, but you can still find copies floating around in vintage record shops.

The other question is "Where is that big suspension bridge in the open of "Texas Country Reporter"?" It's called the Regency Bridge. It's on a dirt road and it's not easy to find. But if you're looking for some extra backroads adventure, it's a trip worth taking. To get to the bridge, take Highway 574 west out of Goldthwaite, Texas, for about 15 miles until Highway 573 intersects the road on your right(north). Continue on 574 just a short distance and you will see a dirt road on your left. Turn left on the dirt road. It will take you south through what's left of Regency and then on to the Regency Bridge which crosses the Colorado River. "The Roads of Texas" atlas is a must for this trip. You'll find Regency on page 100. Good luck and happy traveling.

Bob Phillips

The Ovilla
Information Bureau

If you drive down Main Street in Ovilla, Texas, you can't miss it. It's still sittin' there just like it has been for the better part of fifty years.

It's called Pickard's Store, but it's really a left-over reminder of the way things used to be. Back when Wilson Pickard opened up for business, he was the only mercantile in town. In fact, he had the only telephone around for miles. Folks came in from surrounding farms to pick up groceries and check their messages from relatives. If you needed to leave word with someone you left it with Wilson. Pickard's Store was the focal point of the community.

Stop #1
Ovilla, TX

Today you'll find a new Ovilla, with gas station grocery shops and tract housing popping up like weeds. Yep, things have changed in this once rural town. Little Ovilla is growing up. Progress has found the tiny town tucked away on a backroad. But somehow in the midst of it all, Pickard's store has managed to hang on.

It's just one room and the floors slope to the walls. The sodas in the cooler are sold by the bottle, but the conversation is free.

For as long as anybody can remember, Wilson has been trading news right along side the bread and crackers in the middle aisle. Everyday, little by little, old friends and old codgers who make up the so-called Ovilla Information Bureau shuffle in, pull up a soda box and take on the major issues of the day. When we stopped in, Wilson, Thurman and Mr. Bruce were just getting started.

We asked what they talked about, and we got an earful.

11

"Oh, politics and farmin', mostly politics --
and farmin'," Mr. Bruce says.

They talk about the way things were and the
way things used to be -- who's president and
who ought to be president, and how taxes are
going to kill us all. Mostly they talked, and
mostly we listened.

"You know Bob, long time ago they'd gather
here and there was only one type, and that was
Democrats," Wilson says. "Now then you can't

Bob sitting around with the fellows at Ovilla Store.

tell. You can't tell who's who and what's what.
It's just all together different."

There's one other thing they talk about here --
progress, and how it's turned Ovilla on its ear
almost overnight.

See, Ovilla sits right in the path of the new superconducting super collider, and construction and new housing has become as much a part of the landscape as the cattle and mesquite trees.

"Where I live the development is coming toward me to the point I can hear the tractors and see the black smoke on the back side of my place where they're building for a planned development, and that means I'm next. There's nothing I can do about it, they're just comin' on," Thurman says with a bit of sadness. "I don't want to sell, but what can I do."

Yes, the high tech world of science and technology just might change little Ovilla. Word is, the folks with the government are making some pretty high dollar offers for the farms that dot the countryside. But Wilson says even the scientists are welcome to stop in, find a seat and add their thoughts to the topic of the day.

The Ovilla Information Bureau likely won't solve all the major issues of our time. They won't stem the tide of progress sweeping through their town. But they do care about their own piece of history here, and you are always welcome to sit in and enjoy the conversation.

Oh, if you're wondering what happened to Thurman's farm, a developer offered him a million dollars cash for the land. He turned it down.

You can find the Pickard's General Store at 705 Main Street in Ovilla about 20 minutes south of Dallas on FM 664. They are open Monday through Friday 7am to 6pm and on Saturdays 7am to 5pm. 214-515-3311

"Where I live the development is coming toward me to the point I can hear the tractors and see the black smoke..."
-Thurman

Lions and Tigers and Cougars...Oh My!

Stop #2
Boyd, TX

One thing you develop when you spend time traveling Texas, if you don't have it already, is a respect for wildlife. Over the years we've seen just about every kind the state has to offer. We've also developed a special respect for those who see to it that the Texas wildlife survives without harm. We've visited wildlife sanctuaries from Texarkana to El Paso, Childress to Brownsville. Some are big operations run by big organizations, others work out of someone's kitchen. All need more money and more help and more understanding. Most do the best they can with what little they have and do make a difference. One of the most impressive, as far as we're concerned, is located in Boyd, Texas. It's called the Texas Exotic Feline Foundation and is run by our friends Robert and Gene Reitnauer.

When Gene talked Robert into letting her bring home a leopard more than ten years ago, little did she know it was the small beginning to something very big. Four tigers, three lions and nineteen other big cats later (as of this writing), Robert and Gene are the founders of a foundation for fancy felines and run the largest big cat sanctuary in the state.

"Big cats were here before we were," Robert says. "Unfortunately, there are parts of Africa where the lion will be extinct in 20 years. It's going to be a very ugly world someday with just people, a few dogs, horses and cows."

Make no mistake, big cats are <u>never</u> pets, though some people don't seem to understand that. People buy the cats when they are cute, cuddly cubs...then, in a year, they outweigh

14

them and are eating them out of house and home and don't mind like the family dog. And that's where the Reitnauers come in. The cats brought to the Texas Exotic Feline Foundation are often sick, undernourished and abused. It is very common for law enforcement agencies to deliver big cats they have confiscated in drug raids. Seems the sick people who deal drugs to the world have a thing for big cats, so the cats are taken into custody at the same time as the drug dealers. When that happens, the cats need a home.

Robert Reitnauer with one of his exotic cats.

"A lot of people think we are crazy to fool with them, but these animals have no other place to go," Robert says. "We realized that

15

early on and came up with the idea of a sanctuary."

One ironic twist to the story...for fifteen years Robert Reitnauer was a big game hunter in Africa. For whatever reason, he will no longer do that. Instead, he captures the majesty of these animals in bronze. Robert is an artist and the proceeds from his work help keep the doors open at the sanctuary.

It takes a lot of money to operate the Texas Exotic Feline Foundation, money raised entirely from donations. Like most animal organizations, there are no tax dollars, no United Way funds to count on. Robert, Gene and a handful of volunteers keep the place going and take no salaries for their work.

"It's going to be a very ugly world someday with just people, a few dogs, horses and cows."
-Robert Reitnauer

You can help, too. Obviously, donations are always welcome. But the Reitnauers can always use an extra hand. So, if you'd like to visit the big cats at the Texas Exotic Feline Foundation, you're always welcome at the foundation in Boyd. Understand, though, that you will be put to work while you're visiting. If you're like most folks we've talked to, you'll make the trip more than once.

They are on Highway 114 west, 3 miles from Rhome and 3 miles from Boyd. They conduct tours by appointment only so you need to call ahead. They do ask for a minimum donation of $15 for adults and $5 for children under 12. 817-433-2378

The Chairman and CEO of Snow Cones

Now there are snow cones and then there are snow cones. Once you pass puberty you realize that some are more like soft snow than others. These don't really crunch when you bite into them, rather they kind of mush into your mouth...a lot like snow. But when you're a kid that really doesn't matter. What matters most is the person who sells you the snow cone. That person is a giant, a true hero and a friend.

Stop #3
Gainesville, TX

When Billy Sims was growing up near Gainesville, he always appreciated the simple things. When the lazy days of summer got hot and the sun was high overhead, Billy Sims collected enough empties to cash in at the grocery store and then headed for the local snow cone stand for a strawberry syrup on shaved ice. Billy Sims loved life, simplicity and snow cones.

That Huckleberry mentality didn't last long. Billy grew up and wanted to be a success. He wanted to climb the corporate ladder and, some day, be the President and CEO of his own company. His biggest desire was to have lots of money and do as he pleased, so he studied hard, earned two bachelors and a masters degree, and climbed the corporate ladder. But when he got near the top rung Billy Sims didn't like the view. Billy longed for the simple days of his childhood. He longed for the snow cone days.

Today Billy Sims is President and CEO of his own company. He has a dollar in his pocket and he is, by his own definition, a big success. Billy Sims owns and operates The Snow Cone Stand in Gainesville, Texas.

Snow cones are a seasonal thing, so Billy spends the winter months on the beach. He thinks about life, studies the words of Henry David Thoreau and plans for the next summer at The Snow Cone Stand.

"Not much to it, just ice and syrup," he says. "But that's the physical part, the logistics of being a snow cone man. I also pay close attention to the mental part."

The mental part? Yessiree. You see, Billy Sims still remembers what it was like to be a kid. He remembers that, to most kids, the snow cone itself really doesn't matter that much. What matters is the person who sells it to you. That person is a giant, a true hero and a friend. So Billy Sims talks to, and, more importantly, listens to every kid who walks up and plunks down a buck. And also those who can't. He hears their hopes and their dreams and their problems. He watches them grow up. He is their friend.

"Really, though, I'm only working toward one goal: to be able to fit all my worldy possessions into a knap- sack..."
-Billy Sims

There are lots of places you can get a snow cone, but the trip to Gainesville is well worth the time. You'll get to meet Billy Sims, President and CEO of his own company. And, while you're there, you'll get a pretty good snow cone.

You'll find The Snow Cone Stand on the corner of California and Grand in Gainesville. He opens shop about the first of April and closes about the time school rolls around. He's closed on Sundays.

18

It's Nuts.
The World's Only Pecan Art Museum

Let's get something straight. The popular Texas nut is called a "pah - 'cahn". It's not a "pee'- can". Everybody in Texas already knows that, but you never know who's going to be reading this or where it might end up, so we need to have an understanding about the proper pronunciation of this word. This story would never work if you pronounced it "pee'- can". It would just be silly.

Stop #4
Denton, TX

Come to think of it, this one is already silly, or at least it borders on silly. But that's okay because we can all use a little silliness now and then. Anyway, there are all kinds of things you can do with Texas pecans. You can, of course, make a pecan pie with them. It's a little tricky if you don't know what you're doing cause those things can turn to sugar real quick and get hard as a hockey puck, but once you get the hang of it, well, there are few things as heavenly as a properly prepared pecan pie. You can add pecans to just about anything. Brownies, ice cream, Chinese food and fruit salad. Just about anything tastes better with pecans.

B. W. Crawford is a man who knows his pecans, and well he should. He's seen thousands, maybe millions of them in the last decade or so. He's seen every shape and size from big ole paper shells to tiny natives, he's seen every shape and size of pecans.

"I buy and sell pecans," he explains. "I have a custom cracking business, so I've seen bushels and bushels of pecans and cracked thousands of pounds of them. I have access to quite a few pecans."

Bushels of pecans had passed unnoticed through B.W.'s clanky old pecan cracker until, one day, B.W. started seeing things no one had ever seen before.

"Through the years I've been watching these different sizes and shapes of pecans go through my machines," he says. "I got to recognizing some of them as certain people, the shapes and all, it looked like people's heads. After a few

George Bush as a pecan.

years of looking at them, I started painting faces on them."

Today B.W. does more than paint faces on pecans...he puts together whole bodies, tiny pecan people. B.W. came up with a nutty way to take a crack at something he calls "pecan art". He had never done artwork before, had only picked up a paintbrush to whitewash the fence. Still, like a sculptor says of the stone, "the face was already there...all I had to do was let it out", so B. W. lets the people out of the pecans. Today, B. W. has broken out of his shell in a big way. In fact, this Pecan Picasso has created so many pecan art figures, he has now opened what he says is the world's only pecan art museum.

"I call it the world's only pecan art museum because I don't know of any others," he said.

The world's only pecan art museum has just about everything...and everyone...you can think of: George Bush and Dan Quayle, E.T., Marilyn Monroe, David Letterman, Regis and Kathy Lee, Cher, Elvis, Christ and Johnny Carson.

"I've even got one of my wife and myself," he says. "Most people don't believe it's actually pecans. I've even got a recreation of The Last Supper." John Wayne, Groucho Marx, the list goes on and on. The trick is just finding the right nut. B.W. says he and the pecans are the right nuts.

The World's Only Pecan Art Museum is located at 138 Chaparral Estates in Denton. Admission is free and they are open whenever B.W. is around. Please call before you come so they'll be ready for you. 817-321-3461

"Through the years I've been watching these different sizes and shapes of pecans go through my machines...I got to recognizing some of them as certain people..."
-B.W. Crawford

Harvesting a Cash Crop of Memories in Ennis

Stop #5
Ennis, TX

We're often times finding places that'll set you back a few years...places that'll conjure up pictures from great-gramma's family album...places where new generations can get a taste of old fashioned living and, perhaps, even older, time-honored values. Travel with us long enough and you'll find that we make our way back to the farm a lot. I guess that's because, for us, the farm has always painted a Norman Rockwell picture of simpler times.

Simpler, though, usually translates "harder". In grampa's day, the farm meant dirty fingernails, sweaty overalls and 40 acres of plowing at the wheel of an old John Deere, if he was lucky, 40 acres of plowing with a team of mules if he was not. In grampa's day, men had names like Cal and Frank and Joe and they farmed by the Almanac and the seat of their pants. Gramma and Grampa's farm will set you back a few years and conjure up pictures from the family album - it'll give new generations a taste of old fashioned living and time-honored values. But, the question is, who wants to go back there? Who among us wants to leave the air conditioned aisles of the supermarket in exchange for a trip to the family farm of yesterday?

The answer: Karen Weaver. Karen wants to go back to the old days of the family farm when times were tough, but so were the people. And she has. She's made the trip all the way back to the farm of the 1930s when there was no such thing as an air conditioned combine with a tape player and television on-board. She's made the trip back to a time when you worked with your hands and everybody pitched together to get the job done. Karen Weaver has returned to the farm, and you're invited to come along, too.

It all started when Steve and Karen Weaver's daughters, Dora and Kora, cashed in the milk money they'd been saving for college and bought a couple of draft horses. Karen thinks the girls have a pioneer spirit in their genes that makes them love livestock and the outdoors. Those horses started a family love affair with another time.

These days, it's more than just Steve and Karen, Dora and Kora who work the Weaver family farm in Ennis, Texas. Folks travel from all over the state just to get the chance to be field hands. They come to help with the

Harvest time at the Weaver farm.

> *"This is what this country was built on, hard work like this by hard working people like these."*
> *-Karen Weaver*

harvest, to put 75 acres of oats in the barn - short work with an air conditioned John Deere. But people don't come here to do it the easy way because then they'd miss the music of a 1930 thrasher and a close, personal relationship with a pitchfork.

"Everybody's got to get their crop in someway," Karen says. "We just decided to do it this way for our own personal pleasure. Then we started thinking 'hey, if I like this, well, maybe somebody else likes this.' So we decided to invite the whole county. To me, that's romance. Real romance."

So people just show up at the Weaver family farm on the weekend of the oat harvest. Some are old friends and family. Some are strangers who long to see that thrasher working, to hear the music it makes. They're here to prove that people can still work together and help each other. Strangers stand next to strangers working with pitchforks, putting blisters next to the handle. Karen says its just an "old timey farming thang."

"There's a guy up there stacking," she explains, "now, get this, would ya. He's eighty-five! Now how about that for shaming ya? Eighty-five! This is what this country was built on, hard work like this by hard working people like these."

You, too, can be a part of that old timey farming thang if you're not scared of hard work. The Weavers are off Highway 34 on Ensign Rd. There is no house number. Binding days are usually the first week of June and thrashing begins two weeks or so after that. Call before you come out to help. 214-875-4777

The Majestic Theatre -- the "Real" Last Picture Show

In downtown Will Point, Texas, the railroad tracks cut a path right straight through the center of town.

The trains don't stop here anymore. Most folks here don't remember a time when they ever did.

But there are plenty of reminders of the way things used to be in Wills Point.

Squint hard and look close and you can decifer what's left of the old signs on the sides of forgotten businesses. Chipped and faded paint on crusty bricks reveal a bank, a soda fountain, and a dry goods store.

Back in the twenties, Wills Point even had a family owned theatre, (make that *picture show* if you were born before 1950).

It was called the Majestic and it sat not fifty yards from the edge of the tracks. Lucky for us, some things never change.

Karl Lybrand owns and operates the Majestic Theatre just like his daddy did, and his daddy before that. In fact, the Majestic is the oldest independently owned theater in continuous operation in the state -- probably in the nation.

They still show first run movies here, and a seat will cost you a mere $2.50 -- not a bad investment to sit inside a piece of theatre history.

"We're not in this for the money", Karl says, "it's as important to this community as it is to me. There's only a few places in the world like this left."

On cool summer nights when the train roars through town, Karl rushes to the lobby to

Stop #6
Wills Point, TX

"There's only a few places in the world like this left."
- *Karl Lybrand*

perform an odd family ritual.

In a mad scramble, you'll hear the whap, whap, whap sound of closing doors as Karl hurries to beat the oncoming train.

See, Karl saves money relying on mother nature's ventilation, but the problem is the darn trains drown out the sound of the movie. After a toe-tapping wait, Karl swings the doors open again. It's a sight you just won't see at your big city 50 screen have-it-all theatre, but it's just

Karl Lybrand, owner/operator of the Majestic Theater.

another night out at the picture show for the folks in Wills Point.

The Majestic Theatre is located on Highway 80 just north of the railroad tracks in Wills Point. You can bank on the fact that everything there will cost about half of what it would in the big city. Call 903-873-8140 to find out what's playing when and for how much.

Brewers Bell Museum

Stop and think about the ways we use bells. Bells sound alarms, call us together, and signal beginnings and endings. From doorbells to my personal favorite -- the dinner bell, the ringing of a bell means something to everyone.

But Virginia Bell Brewer (that's really her name), gets more excited about bells than anyone we've ever met. So excited, in fact, that Virginia Brewer collected so many bells, that she had to build a museum just to house them all, and you're invited to come visit.

Stop #7
Canton, TX

The sign out on the highway says there are over 3,000 bells on display. At last count, Virginia had 3,131 to be exact. They come from all fifty states and more than seventy countries around the world. Virginia started this accumulation of carillons more than fifty years ago, and she's never slowed down since.

"I liked bells because of my name," Virginia says. "Then in 1940, my sister gave me a china bell. Little did she realize what she was starting."

From tiny tinkling bells, to the gong-like ring of big brass bells, Virginia has a bell in just about every shape, sound and size. There are bells made from colorful crystal, polished glass, china, clay, and even silver and bronze.

The oldest bell in Virginia's collection dates back to about 1337 B.C., proof that bells have been around a while.

Amassing this amazing collection has taken Virginia Brewer almost a lifetime. She's belt high in bells. But as interesting as it seems, the little bell museum does not draw huge crowds. On a typical day, only a few passing tourists trickle in and take the grand tour.

Virginia does have a catalog listing every bell she has and where she got it, but she rarely needs to reference it. With just a quick glance, Virginia can tell you a story about every bell in the house -- where it came from and how it got here.

"That's what I like the most," Virginia says. "Being able to share the beauty of my bells and the stories that go along with them."

"I liked bells because of my name," Virginia says. *"Then in 1940, my sister gave me a china bell. Little did she realize what she was starting."*
-Virginia Bell

We could go on and on telling you about how interesting Virginia Brewer's little bell museum is and why bells are so important to us, but it was John F. Kennedy who said it best:

"Bells mark significant events in men's lives. Birth and death. War and peace. Bells summon people to take note of things which effects their life and the destiny of people."

You will find Virginia Bell Brewer's Bell Museum on Highway 64 between I-20 and Canton. She is two miles from the county courthouse. The museum is open from 10am to about 6 Monday through Saturday, and she also opens every first Sunday of the month. Tours are $1 for kids and $2 for adults, but a big group can go for half price. The tour lasts about an hour. 903-567-4632

Making Mud Pies --
the Pine Mills Potters

They say that over the last half century more and more people have moved out of the country and into the big city. We're happy to report that there are plenty around who have moved the other way. Like the folks who call themselves the Pine Mills Potters.

There are other things Gary and Daphne Hatcher could be doing for a living...he knows the construction business and she's been in sales. But from the day they met in school they knew their lives would end up in clay.

"When we first built our kiln, " Daphne said, "everybody thought we were opening a barbecue stand. When we finally did open and said we were potters there was a lot of curiosity. I'm not sure people knew what a potter was."

Today folks around Pine Mills know very well what a potter is. Folks from town and nearby farms drop by to browse or to watch or just to sit and chat. "I like to tell people we're just stuck in the mud pie stage of development," Daphne said.

When they came to the Piney Woods over a decade ago, Gary and Daphne felt drawn to the place but they didn't know why. Now they think they do. It seems they weren't the first potters to call Pine Mills home.

"We started digging a lake and found chard," Daphne explains. "We said 'stop' because we didn't want anything else disturbed."

What they had found was the remains of a kiln dating back to the Civil War. Every broken jar and jug was a piece of the potter's history.

Stop #8
Pine Mills, TX

"I like to tell people we're just stuck in the mud pie stage of development. That's what we still like to do, make mud pies all day long."
-Daphne Hatcher

Gary and Daphne like to think that when you take home a Pine Mills pot, you take home a little piece of east Texas history. Their kiln is fired with East Texas pine, their pottery is made from East Texas clay. Even the handles on their serving trays are made from East Texas muscadine vines wrestled from the trees.

They could have done something different. Gary could have stayed a carpenter. Daphne could have stayed in sales. They could have

Gary and Daphne Hatcher, the Pine Mills potters.

stayed in the city. We're happy to report they did not.

The Pine Mills Potters are located one mile west of the intersection of FM14 and FM49, northwest of Mineola just the other side of Hainesville. They are open 10am to 5pm Monday through Saturday and 1pm to 5pm on Sunday. It's best to call ahead to make sure that someone is there. 214-857-2271

Kitchen's - Hardware and Ham, Ladders and Lunch

When you travel the backroads for a living, you naturally have your favorites. There are some roads that just <u>feel</u> good when you're driving down them. Something about the combination of the scenery, the towns you pass through and even the road itself. One of my favorites is Highway 80 as it runs east out of Dallas through East Texas.

The best place to catch 80 is just outside Terrell where you ease off I-20 and into a different frame of mind. These are real Texas farming towns along here...Wills Point, Edgewood, Fruitvale, Elmo. The road has just the right amount of dips and curves to keep things interesting and the towns are spaced just the right distance apart. The blacktop is plenty wide so you don't have to worry about getting caught behind a slow moving tractor and the railroad tracks run parallel most of the way so you can count the cars and wonder where they're off to. About the time you get to Mineola (named by some railroad folks for their daughters, Minnie and Ola) you'll want to pull over and grab a Coke and stretch your legs. But watch out. This town has a way of snaring newcomers and passers through and keeping them. It's happened before.

Jim and Bunny Young liked their life in the big city just fine. Or, so they thought. That was before they got a taste of Mineola and before they found "it". "It" was a 5000 foot 1890s era hardware store built by Dave Kitchen, Sr., complete with pot-bellied stove and 1903 hand-pulled Otis rope elevator.

Stop #9
Mineola, TX

"We had bought a weekend place here and it got harder and harder to go back to Dallas," Jim says. "Then Bunny saw this store was available. She had never even been in a hardware store, but we bought it and she started running it."

A hundred years have passed down Broad Street since Kitchen's first opened for business proclaiming "if we don't have it, you don't need it." Today you can still get all kinds of nuts and bolts, in bulk or one at a time, ten

Jim Young serving lunch at Kitchen's Hardware.

penny nails and 20 gauge wire. They've even got horn weights and something called a blab. Bunny Young runs the hardware store.

"I had a little screwdriver in my kitchen drawer somewhere, that was the extent of my hardware knowledge," Bunny says.

Today she'll cut you a piece of plastic pipe or show you where to find the right size hinge pin.

But that's not all you can get at Kitchen's. Right there in the front of the store they'll serve you up an ice cream cone or fix you a ham and cheese on rye. Kitchen's doesn't just have hardware. Kitchen's has a kitchen. And a full blown delicatessen.

"It seemed like the only thing you couldn't get here was lunch," Jim says. "So, we added that. And Bunny and I have an agreement. I don't know anything about hardware and she can't cook, so I'll make your sandwich and she'll find your lockwashers. People who don't know naturally ask me about hardware and I usually say 'you'll have to ask my wife.' "

Whether you drop in for a hacksaw and hammer or a turkey on wheat, Kitchen's is well worth it. Jim and Bunny Young will serve you either or both with a smile.

To get to Kitchen's Hardware and Deli, take Highway 80 east to 119 East Broad in Mineola. They're open daily from 8 to 5, closed Sundays. The phone number is 903-569-2664.

"If we don't have it, you don't need it."
-*Kitchen's Hardware Store*

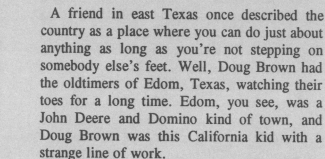

The Day the Potter Came to Edom -- and Changed Everything

Stop #10
Edom, TX

"Folks here were curious about what I did for a living...the farmers were getting pretty suspicious."
-Doug Brown

A friend in east Texas once described the country as a place where you can do just about anything as long as you're not stepping on somebody else's feet. Well, Doug Brown had the oldtimers of Edom, Texas, watching their toes for a long time. Edom, you see, was a John Deere and Domino kind of town, and Doug Brown was this California kid with a strange line of work.

"Folks here were curious about what I did for a living," Doug says. "I was making things in the back of my shop and selling them out the front and lots of people were driving in from the city and parking the Mercedes and Cadillacs along the street. The farmers were getting pretty suspicious."

These days the Exxon station is about the only business north of Main Street that doesn't make what it sells. Doug "Potter" Brown can usually be found throwing (honest, that's what they call it) clay at his wheel with a group of visitors watching as he works.

But there's plenty more in Edom. Next door Zeke Zewick and Marty Flanagan are turning out sculpture -- belts and buckles and serving implements made from leather, bone and brass. There are others here, too. A whole cache of artists who have joined "Potter" Brown to create one of the quaintest east Texas artist communities. The signs of the times in Edom are the ones advertising weaving and leather, pottery and antiques.

Another sign of the times is the keys to the volunteer fire department hanging from the wall in a craftsmen's shop. Seems folks in Edom got pretty excited about all the artistic goings on in their little town, and today the potter and others are part of the family. Edom even has an annual festival -- The Edom Art Fair, where one weekend each year the town of a couple or three hundred swells to more than 10,000 and Edom artists are joined by craftspeople from around the country.

Although most of the Edom shops are open

Doug Brown, the California potter, who came to Edom.

during the week, there are no set hours, so it's always a good idea to call ahead to make sure somebody will be around.

Edom is located 80 miles east of Dallas on FM 279 between Canton and Tyler. Although you can visit Edom anytime, the fair serves as a showcase for the artists. The fair is held in the 2 acre meadow behind the artists workshops on Main street. The art fair is on the last weekend in September and runs from 10am to 6pm on Saturday and Sunday. Admission is free. 903-852-6473

The Whirlygig Man

The 9-15 cuts through the East Texas country side like a red tail hawk coming down on a field mouse. It doesn't even slow up when it blows through Hawkins. And folks here rarely notice its passing. It's just part of life in a town missed by the interstate and happy for it. People in Hawkins are content with a slower pace, pleased to leave the hurry-up world to big city slickers and their cellular society. Life here is simple and that's the way Don Taylor and his neighbors want it.

Don Taylor is satisfied. When you think about it, that's quite a thing to be. How many of us can make such a claim? Satisfaction means more than just being content. It means it's all come together for you, not necessarily the way you planned, but in a way that makes sense of life. And that's what Don does best...makes sense of life, albeit in a strange and quirky way none of the rest of us could possibly understand. Then, that's probably our loss. After all, Don is the one who is satisfied.

"A person's got to get into his own groove," Don says. "And sometimes he gets a reputation for being unconcerned or even lazy. But I've been trying to answer the question 'what am I?' all my life and finally I've found the answer: I'm just me."

Don is not unconcerned and he's not what you would call lazy. He even owns a business in Hawkins, though it's certainly different from the way most folks make a living. He's the designer and manufacturer of a funny contraption that looks something like a windmill or a whirlygig or even a weather vane. Don says it's all of those and none of those. He calls them "windaids" and his yard is crammed full of them. They are delicately balanced machines which turn with the slightest breeze, and when the 9-15 blows by Don's house, it sets off a heck of a commotion. He spends hours building each one and sells them for a song. Still, Don Taylor, alias "Windy Mills", is a very rich man.

"Rich in mind, but not in my pocket book," he says. "I gave up on getting rich and started building my wind machines. It's more fun. 'Cause I 'bout decided all you're going to do is get by, and if you can get by being happy and have a satisfied mind then you're the richest person in the world."

One more thing about Don "Windy Mills" Taylor. He's a poet.

He writes about everyday life but in a way most of us probably wouldn't dream of, though we could certainly relate. Don's even got one about his crazy wind machines. Or maybe it's really just about being different. Or maybe it's autobiographical.

You'll find Don Taylor in Hawkins, Texas, at the corner of Moore Street and Highway 14. Just look for the "windaids" on the lawn. He welcomes visitors to his shop anytime, he just asks that you call before you stop by. 903-769-4134

"I've been trying to answer the question 'what am I' all my life and finally I've found the answer: I'm just me."
-Windy Mills

FINAL CHAPTER

Where will you be,
> Whenever the "book folds shut"?
Will you be like the most;
> Digging deeper in a rut,
Or leave an indelible mark,
> On a world full of marks,
With the "bulls eye", in lifes target,
> Blind with your darts?
Lifes final chapter,
> You still yet have to read.
You must write it, yourself;
> Make it a good one, indeed.

Stand out of the way,
> When you close shut, this book,
'Cause closing won't take as long,
> As my writing it took.
If you let this little book,
> Fold its cover on you,
You could "end up" being---
> JUST another rhyme, too.

Don Taylor

Don Taylor, otherwise known as Windy Mills, in his front yard.

Crooked Wind Mill

I once built a crooked windmill,
And put it with a group of straight ones.
It never wanted to do much of nothing,
But sit on its crooked buns.

The poor old thing had a mind of its own,
But I had no way of knowing.
The only time it wanted to turn
Was when the wind was never blowing.

One calm spring day it began to turn
While all the others were sleeping.
I'd have never known it I hadn't been
Just around the corner a peeking.

I admire a man with a mind of his own,
And the same thing goes for a windmill.
So now I keep it inside my shop
And the dang thing never sits still.

If you know someone that folks call lazy,
Because he seldom gets "on the move"
Maybe the winds of life are a little too strong
For him to ever get in the groove.

Don Taylor

Farmer Bart and Farmer Brent Harvesting Their Heritage in Hooks

Stop #12
Hooks, TX

Early morning in the farm country. The sun spreads out over dew-damp fields and the ground sparkles and the first warm rays of the day turn everything to gold for a brief, magical moment. You want to stop and drink it in, because it doesn't last nearly long enough and fewer and fewer people are left out here to see it at all.

Brent Ramage is in his mid 30s. Brother Bart is three years older. Together they run the family farm, 600 acres spreading back off the banks of the Red River near the town of Hooks. Back when the brothers were born, one in every three families lived on a farm. Today its fewer than one in fifty.

The Ramage boys do not run your conventional family farm. You will not find a thrasher or combine on the place. What you will find are fields full of pecans...and pumpkins...and blueberries. Crops without price supports, crops that count on customers who simply want the real thing for a delicious homemade pie.

Now money isn't exactly falling off the trees these days. Any farmer, and most anybody else, will tell you that. So what you do, if you're a family like the Ramages, is you take the big barn that was home only to owls and alley cats, kick them outside and open the Ramage Country Store and sell those delicious pie fixins right there on the home place. So far, in spite of a tough economy, the Ramages are making it.

It's a unique concept, really. Raising crops that people want instead of not raising crops because the government pays you not to raise them. The Ramages have a rule: grow only the stuff that costs less to produce than the selling price. It's called profit, supply and demand, the American way. The Ramage brothers are pretty good at it, but they have no misconception about who they are working for.

"You work hard and do the best you can to produce the best you can, but never make the

The Ramage brothers on their farm.

mistake of thinking you own the land," one of the brothers says. "You don't own the land, the land owns you. No one owns the land. You might have title to it, but a hundred years from now the only mark on the land will be how you cared for it...that's just one of nature's rules.

The land has been here for millions of years and we're just here for a very short time."

When you visit Ramage Farm and the Ramage Country Store, you'll find a rustic barn straight out of the 1930s. It was built in 1930 as a home for mules that were used to work the cotton fields, and on a clear day you can see all the way to the Red River from the balcony. Below is the pecan orchard with trees that were grafted in 1929 and still produce today. During the fall of the year the place is covered in pumpkins. In front is a blueberry patch where you can pick your own in June and July.

There's even a hay loft where you can enjoy a cold drink and take in the sights, sounds and smells of this family farm. They'll even share family recipes with you, and the coffee is always hot.

And, if you're lucky enough to be there early in the day, all the better. Remember: in the early morning, the sun spreads out over the dew-damp fields and the ground sparkles and the first rays of the day turn everything to gold for a brief, magical moment.

Ramage Farms is located 4.5 miles north of Hooks, Texas, on Farm Road 560, just off Interstate 30. They offer field trips in October and farm tours by request if they have some time to spare. The store is open 8am to 5pm Monday through Friday and 8am to noon on Saturdays. 903-547-6187

"You don't own the land, the land owns you...that's just one of nature's rules."
-Brent Ramage

Milton Watts --
The Piney Woods Poet

If you're looking for a place to go fishing and camping, few places in Texas rival the beauty and majesty of the Piney Woods. Each day, in the pre-dawn stillness, long before the recreational campers awake, the natives of these woods and hollows begin their daily chores.

Milton Watts is a native. His family came to the Piney Woods before the pines did, before Lake O'The Pines was here, before the weekend cottages. He grew up when the dirt dared anyone to make a living off it, when moonshining was a social endeavor and a dollar in your pocket made you a very rich man. Times have changed, as they inevitably do. Lake O'The Pines was created and overnight the Watts family acres became more profitable just sitting under water than they ever were cracking under the sun. Today Milton Watts owns a fishing camp and trailer park. Where his daddy once plowed the soil, Milton now sells bait and tends to tourists. It's a part he never really wanted to play.

For almost 30 years Milton has catered to fishermen and weekend tourists at Island View Landing. Frivolous as it may be, selling fish bait has made Milton wealthy but not happy. He's seen his heritage of honest hard labor slip away like the morning fog. The soil that his parents fought to nurture is now at the bottom of a lake he never wanted and there's nothing to show for the sweat his mother and father shed to make something of this place except for the musings of a country boy turned poet.

Milton has become something of a poet laureate of East Texas, chronicling the life and

Stop #13

Lake O'The Pines, TX

"I got to noticing people would come down here from the high pressure atmosphere of the city and they'd slow down and enjoy life."
-Milton Watts

43

"I see the lake water caressing the sandy loam

Along ancestral acres I've always called home

I figure fate has flagged the way

Here I am, here I have been, here I'll stay."

-Milton Watts

Milton Watts, the east Texas poet.

times of his people in a way few others can match. Folks have grown accustomed to his extemporaneous recitals on the end of the dock at Island View Landing. A Milton Watts poem is well worth the trip, even if you don't catch any fish.

You can see Milton, buy some bait and hear his poetry by visiting Island View Landing at Lake O'The Pines east of Jefferson off FM726 on FM1968. Just follow the signs. They are open every day of the year, even Christmas, daylight to dusk. 903-777-4161

WORD FORCE

The speech and expression
       that I esteem -
Flows from it's source
       like a stream.

Honest, sincere,
       and from the heart -
Truths not shaped to pretentious forms
       by aping art.

But, in words falling forth freely -
       blunt and precise - yet - not pristine.
Like strong currents moving forcefully, muddily -
       still, somehow, clean.

Words expressed simply for all to hear,
       or if written see -
Dislodging sham
       as coursing waters displace debris.

                         Milton Watts

Historic Jefferson --
Bed, Breakfast, and a
Whole Lot of History

Stop #14
Jefferson, TX

There are some towns in this state that just pop up and grab you, reach out and nab you. Jefferson, Texas, has got to be at the top of the list.

It's that kind of town, Jefferson. The kind that will invite you in for a day and take you back a century. It's a town with a story to tell.

Historic Old Jefferson they call it. Historic because a lot of famous folks have been here or lived here. Old because many of its homes go back a hundred years or more. If you bothered to count them, you'd find 70 historical markers in this town, dating back to before the Civil War.

Fact is, you can't walk a block without strolling back a century. In Sam Houston's day, Jefferson was a booming river port and cotton center. People came by the thousands to seek their fortune here.

In its day, Jefferson was a roudy, raucus river town -- port of entry and exit for both people and goods combined. It was home, they say, to paddle wheelers and the wheeler dealers. It was a town that would never die. That was before the river changed and the water dropped and Jefferson almost dried off the map.

Today Lexy Palmore makes a living off Jefferson's boom and bust story. Lexy is a riverboat captain. One of only a few woman licensed to pilot the big barges on the Mississippi. Instead, Lexy chooses to show Jefferson to tourists from the seat of a tiny boat that makes its way up and down Big Cypress Bayou. Lexy explains how Jefferson once was, then wasn't, and now is again. She invites visitors to be a part of her town for a day.

There are plenty of things to do in Jefferson -- lots of places to explore. You can spend a day just brousing the stores and antique shops. Take the historical tour and visit The Captain's Castle, The House of Seasons, or The Freeman Plantation. Kick back at Auntie Skinner's Riverboat Club. Or have an incredible meal at the Stillwater Inn, The Black Swan, or any number of great restaurants. If you want to spend more than a day, Jefferson is the king of bed and breakfast lodging. There are several fine, old historic hotels like The Excelsior House where U.S. Presidents and captains of industy have spent the night. Rumor has it The Excelsior is haunted, and in fact Steven Speilberg once picked up his entire film crew and left in the middle of the night because he claims the ghosts kept him awake.

Jefferson is located on Highway 59 north of Marshall. Tourist Information is located at 1026 South Polk St. They are open from 10am to 2pm. You can call them at 903-665-1665 or you can call the Chamber of Commerce at 903-665-2672.

"In its day, Jefferson was a roudy, raucus river town -- port of entry and exit for both people and goods combined."

Mann Perry, The Fish Finder of Caddo Lake

Stop #15
Caddo Lake, TX

Deep in East Texas is a place where the pines turn to cypress, where Spanish Moss falls from the heavens and the crappie practically jump into your boat. Welcome to Caddo Lake, the largest natural lake in the south -- and Mann Perry's home.

Mann Perry says he's "kind of self-employed". He's a fishing guide, a pro with a pole, and he knows every lily pad on Caddo. Just about every morning for almost 50 years he's left the dock at Johnson's ranch long before sunrise with a couple of tourists or wanna-be fishermen in tow.

Hours later, he's back with a mess of crappie and a boatful of smiling faces. Mann could be Caddo's foremost expert at finding fish and pleasing people, and he does it all with a beat up boat and a cane pole.

"Folks was meant to fish with a cane," Mann tells us. "You can use all kinds of fancy rods and reels, they've even got things that tell you how deep the water is and where all the fish are hidin'. But I don't use any of that stuff. I don't need it."

While Mann Perry may take the mystery out of fishing, there's not much he can do about the mystery of Caddo Lake. Some folks claim it's haunted. That's partly because Caddo is more like a Florida swamp than a Texas Lake. The cypress trees, the Spanish Moss and the critters that could be lurking just below the surface all create a spooky feeling. To the newcomer it all looks the same. It's easy to get lost. It's easy to lose your way.

Names like Hog Wallow, Alligator Thicket and Red Belly on the occasional signpost attempt to make sense of this place. But without someone like Mann Perry to guide you through the maze of waterways, you'll probably get lost.

"There's stories about folks who thought they knew the way and were never heard of again," Mann says with a slight grin. "Don't know if they're true, but it ain't never happened to me. I guess I just know what I'm doing. But I still don't like to be out here after dark."

Lots of folks agree. Almost fifty years, six kids and a whole lot of crappie signal the success of Mann Perry. He's been offered jobs on dry land, even moved to the city once for a few months, but he heard the crappie calling, and he made his way back to Caddo.

You can book Mann Perry for a morning on Caddo Lake by calling Johnson Ranch at 903-789-3213. To get there take highway 43 to FM 2198 heading east. That'll run you right into Caddo Lake. Better call well in advance and better do it soon. Mann's been talking about retirement. Says he wants to take some time off and do a little fishing.

"Out here on this lake I'm free. This is where I belong."
-Mann Perry

The End of an Era at The Jonesville Store

Stop #16
Jonesville, TX

Jonesville is one of those east Texas hamlets that's so quiet you want to turn your radio down for fear of waking the little town from a long, peaceful sleep.

For the past 15 years or so, Jonesville hasn't gotten any bigger. Census takers call it negative population growth. Folks here call it the beginning of the end. It all started when the gin shut down. Businesses fell like dominos and folks moved on.

Gone are the hustle bustle days of the T.C. Linsey cotton gin -- the business that cranked out close to 3,000 bales of cotton a year in the 1930s and made Jonesville one of the wealthiest towns in the piney woods.

Today the gin sits cool, quiet and very much closed down. Oh, you might think you hear the boomtown spirit of Jonesville ringing through the gin, but it's just your imagination.

But old habits and old businesses die hard, and the T.C. Linsey and Company General Store is still keeping the doors open and the cash register ringing.

Sam Vaughn is part owner of the place with his brother Tom. Started in 1870, this is truly one of the few remaining real McCoys -- a genu-ine authentic country general store with all the trimmings.

Whether it's sunbonnets or spittoons, carriage parts or kerosene lamps, the T.C. Linsey store has it. It's a throwback to the days when the general store carried everything a person could want, since the next store was probably days away on horseback.

Today folks come from everywhere to get a taste of old country mercantile. Only the store's popularity has kept Jonesville on the map.

The key to the store's success, though, isn't so much what's for sale, but what's not for sale. Sam Vaughn has stuffed this barn of a building with country relics -- antiques that are off limits to the many visitors who like to look and would love to buy. It's a private museum -- a step back into Jonesville's colorful past.

Though time seems to have passed by the store, little else has. Even Hollywood has been here a half a dozen times. And three of those times Sam Vaughn was right where he's been since 1982, behind the counter taking care of customers.

But don't get me wrong, things are slow here -- and getting slower. Seems the Jonesville store has just about everything but a future. With no heirs to take over the place, the store may someday become a forgotten relic along Farm Road 134.

It's a thought Sam can hardly stomach. He's been here all his life. He's watched this place change.

"This place is on a slow go down," Sam told us. "See, we lost the school, lost the depot, lost the post office, and most of our old faithful customers are dead and gone. Five or six grocery salesmen used to call on us, now there's one. And he's fixin' to quit. We used to make a lot of money here. Now we lose it."

But old habits and old businesses die hard, and Tom's determined to stick with it for the sake of the people who trickle in.

"We enjoy people coming in and looking. They get to see all the old things. It makes me want to keep it going for them, which we will as long as we can. I'd like for it to continue

"I'd like for it to continue forever, but I gave up hope for that a long time ago."
-Sam Vaughn

51

forever, but I gave up hope for that a long time ago."

Once Jonesville was an east Texas boom town. Cotton was plentiful and times were good. Today the T.C. Linsey and Company General Store is about all that's left of the town, but Sam and Tom aren't ready to say goodbye. The day they lock the door and walk away, Jonesville will disappear from the roadmap and slip into the pages of history -- lost except for Sam and Tom Vaughn's memories of "the good ole days".

"What I call the good ole days is a thing of the past," Tom says. "It's something to read about and wish it were here again, but it will never be back."

You'll find the T.C. Linsey and Company General Store on Farm Road 134 in Jonesville just west of Waskom in far east Texas. They are open Monday through Saturday 8am to 4:30pm. 903-687-3382

Tom & Sam Vaughn, lifelong merchants.

The Last Sweet Memories at an East Texas Syrup Mill

Shortly after the year's first freezing frost the piney woods of East Texas are quiet. Nature takes a break, resting up for Spring. But on one particular morning, one special day, the peaceful sounds of the wilderness are broken and serenity surrenders to the joyful sounds of people.

Stop #17
Troup, TX

There is excitement in the air. An electric current of anticipation married with the familiar smell of a wood fire. It fills the cool, crisp morning. It is the sweet smell of winter.

It's moments like these that keep us on the backroads. These are the things you take away with you, the times you remember. Friends and neighbors gathered together in scenes like this one, swapping stories and stoking the fire, talking about the way things used to be and the way things ought to be. This is a celebration, a traditional rite of winter. They are gathered here on this one special morning in a pasture of Gary Fields' family farm to cook a ribbon cane syrup.

This, of course, was once a regular occurrence. Today, though, it's not necessary from the point of view of product. You can buy what you need from the neighborhood grocer but then you'd miss the most important part. See, used to be when you wanted something like ribbon cane syrup you made it. And it just made sense for your friends and neighbors to help you and for you to help them. Kind of like raising a barn or harvesting a crop. Everyone pitches in and everyone benefits and in the process friends and neighbors become friendlier and more neighborly. Used to be that way. And, once a year, it still is...at Gary Fields' place.

"We're just trying to preserve a dying tradition, a piece of the past," Gary says. "We just want to keep it alive so people who enjoy seeing it can and for those who never experienced it to have a better understanding of what this life was all about. It's more than just making ribbon cane syrup, it's an important part of life in the old days. It's how people got along together, how they survived."

It was about three or four years ago when Gary Fields dusted off the old syrup cooker tucked away on the family farm. At the time it seemed simple enough, you cut some cane, you squeeze it out, you boil it down. Dozens of hours of hard work later, Gary realized there's a reason the old cooker was left for scrap. The job usually starts at 5 in the morning and lasts 'till dark. There's no stopping or the syrup is lost, good only to feed to the hogs. Cooking good syrup takes time, practice and a whole lot of patience.

"The last year the mill turned before we set it up was 1939. It became a thing of the past and never regained its popularity or its usefulness, probably never will. But it's important to understand it and how it fit into the normal lifestyles of the people who came before us. People stop by who still remember syrup cooking days from their youth and you see their faces light up. It's hard work but still somehow it's a fond remembrance."

If you want to spend a day in the past, stop by the old fashioned syrup making at Gary Fields' family farm. Talk to the folks, sample the syrup. Chew on cane and think about this: simple moments like this one are a great part of

"We're just trying to preserve a dying tradition, a piece of the past..."
-Gary Fields

the socialization of our society in the days before television and cellular phones. This is a dinosaur coming to us straight out of the days when we talked to one another, from a time when we knew our neighbors and cared about people. If you go just to get a bottle of syrup, don't bother to make the drive. It will probably be a waste of your time.

Gary Fields and his family usually break out the syrup on the first weekend in November. They cook all day Friday and Saturday and often part of Sunday, too. Your visit is welcome, but give them a ring to let them know you'll be stopping by. 903-842-4748

Gary Fields cooking sugar cane syrup.

A Collection of Memories Housed in a Village

Stop #18
Nacogdoches, TX

"I just started collecting my families homes to have a place to put my antiques."
- Lera Thomas

Sixty years before the colonies declared their independence from England, Spaniards built a mission in the piney woods along the King's Highway, the main trail to San Antonio. They called the road Camino Real, and they called the town Nacogdoches.

Some say Nacogdoches is the oldest town in Texas, a claim that does not go undisputed. But you can't argue the fact that this town is filled with a colorful history, much of it preserved in a turn-of-the-century village called Millard's Crossing.

It's been a long time since dry goods were sold at the dry goods store, a long time since the barber pole welcomed visitors for a shave and a haircut. It's been a lifetime since lovers courted on the porches of the Victorian homes. Today Millard's Crossing is a collection of memories and a living reminder of Lera Thomas' heritage.

"It's not a park, and it's not a museum," Lera reminds us. "It's the actual homelife of the people who lived in these houses. They are all natural, just as they were a hundred years ago."

Among the homes here is the house Lera grew up in, the home her grandfather lived in, homes of aunts and uncles and cousins, all brought here by a woman who desperately wanted to preserve her past.

"I had been collecting antiques for about forty years, then I realized I didn't have a place to put them, so I just started collecting my family's old homes to make a place for my antiques."

Today Lera Thomas owns and operates her very own village. And you're invited to stop by for a visit. For just $3 you can step back into the 1800s and enjoy the memories of one woman's life.

What you'll find here is a log house built in 1830, the Millard-Lee home built in 1837, the Millard-Burrow home built in 1840, and a church built in 1843, all furnished with items from Lera Thomas' huge antique collection.

If you're lucky, you might get a personal tour

Lera Thomas at home with her antiques.

by Lera herself. Lera's in her nineties now and she will fascinate you with her memories. She's no ordinary lady. When her husband U.S. Congressman Albert Thomas died in office it was Lera who finished out his term, making her the first female member of congress from Texas. She's been friends with four presidents and she made a congressional tour of Vietnam during the war.

Millard's Crossing is open Monday through Friday 9am to 4pm and on Saturday from 7am to 5pm. A tour costs $3 for adults. It is located at 6020 North Street (U.S. Highway 59 north) in Nacogdoches. 409-564-6631

While you're in Nacogdoches, stop by Indian Mound in the 500 block of Mound Street. It's one of the last Caddo Indian burial ground left in this area...at one time there were several.

Note: As we were going to press, Lera Thomas died. However, the folks at the village tell us that her memory will live on, as Millard's Crossing will continue to be open, and you are still welcome to stop by for a visit.

The family church, Millard's Crossing centerpiece.

Pickin' & Grinnin' on the Nacogdoches Square

Just about everyone we meet, just about every place we go is small town. Small towns are where people are used to folks dropping by for a few minutes and staying all day. Life is kind of slow in small towns. Too slow for some. But small towns are just right for pokin' around and seeing what's happening -- or not happening.

For instance, on a Saturday afternoon in downtown Nacogdoches, Texas, there's not much going on unless you listen close to the cool country air and follow the sounds of fiddles and banjos and guitars to The General Mercantile and Old Time String Shop on the square.

"This is what we do around here when there's nothing going on," shop owner Steve Hart says. "Lucky for us, there's never much going on."

Steve Hart is a music man. Guitars, fiddles, dulcimers and stringed instruments of all kinds lay around his cluttered backroom workshop in various states of disrepair. Steve Hart fixes fiddles -- plays them too. Stop by on a Saturday afternoon for a sample.

If you can't count on anything else in this uncertain world, you can count on this -- the Saturday afternoon jam session at the Old Time String Shop. It's just a handful of folks with time on their hands and tunes by the score. If you can keep a beat and can play a lick, congratulations -- you're in the band.

Nobody knows how long this gathering has been going on. Years and years is as close as it gets. Long enough for the young guys to grow

Stop #19
Nacogdoches, TX

"It sure beats sitting in Houston traffic listening to the radio."
-Steve Hart

into their instruments, long enough for the Stephen F. Austin professors who sit in see the college students they taught graduate, marry, and raise kids of their own. They've been coming here a long time -- gathering around the warm wood stove, picking out bluegrass. They all drop in to keep Steve company with the sweet sound of strings.

At times there are crowds so thick there's barely enough room to draw a fiddle bow. Every year bluegrass festivals have pickers and pluckers spilling out into the street. But for all the attention Steve gets, the shop makes very little money. A fiddle bow here, a guitar string there -- just enough to pay the bills and get by.

That's one other thing we like about small towns. In times when there's nothing happening, when there's no sounds of cash registers ringing, no signs of sales, there is almost always the sound of good friends passing good cheer.

You can find Steve Hart's General Mercantile and Old Time String Shop on the south side of the square next to the fire station in Nacogdoches. He's open for business Tuesday though Saturday from 10am to 5pm, but Saturday afternoon is the time to catch the bluegrass jam session. 409-564-8692

Picture This: The History of a Tiny Town on the Walls of a Service Station

Maybe you've wondered how we meet the folks we do, sometimes it's as simple as a fifteen minute oil change.

By our calculations and experience, it takes just about four trips across Texas until it's time to change the oil in our trusty Texas Country suburban. We've stopped for a quick change everywhere from Dime Box to Dalhart, Hooks to Harlingen. Usually in the time it takes to down a Dr. Pepper we're ready to hit the road again, but when we pulled in to Emory's Service Center in Wells, Texas, we stayed for hours.

Emory Williamson has probably seen the underside of every car and pickup in Wells. That's not hard to understand seeing he's been in business for thirty years -- lived here twenty before that. Emory's met a lot of folks in that time, made a lot of memories, too. And for each one of those memories, Emory Williams has a picture.

"I'd been saving pictures for years," Emory says with a grin. "I had a buddy that found a picture of his grandpa in an old trunk, so I put that picture up. First thing you know I had a lot of pictures up in the garage."

If a picture is worth a thousand words, then Emory's got a whole library. What he's got is the unofficial pictorial history of an east Texas logging town dating from the turn of the century.

Next to every tool, tire and car care product, there is a picture -- frozen images of people and places, the familiar and the forgotten. It's a

Stop #20
Wells, TX

"I'd been saving pictures for years...I just like to look back on old memories."
-Emory Williamson

photographic time line of the way things used to be in Wells.

As time goes on the gallery grows. Emory's huge collection has filled his shop, his garage, and two other buildings. There are thousands of pictures of the here and now -- of the then and gone.

Each year on the last Saturday in March Wells has its annual homecoming celebration. Emory's photo display is always the highlight

Emory Williamson surrounded by his pictures.

of the weekend. In one way it's just a collection of pictures, but for Emory Williamson it's a photographic history of a tiny Texas town, a snapshot of one man's memories. You wonder how we meet the folks we do? Sometimes it's a simple as a fifteen minute oil change.

You don't have to wait for homecoming, you can stop by Emory's any day, he'll be happy to show you around. You'll find Emory's Service Center on Highway 69 in Wells, Texas 19 miles north of Lufkin. He is open 7:30am-6:30pm Monday through Friday. If you're planning to get your oil changed anyway, why not make the trip to Wells to have it done? Emory will be happy to let you look around while he adds some 10-W-30. **The best time to go is the last Saturday in March during the Wells Homecoming festivities.**

Wells, Texas, home of Emory's picture museum.

Where Dinosaurs Tread..Or At Least Stand Moscow, TX

Stop #21
Moscow, TX

There have been some peculiar stories come out of the deep, dark East Texas woods. Mostly the folks who tell those stories know they can get away with it because who would want to wander way back in there to check it out? No doubt about it, it's deep in them thar woods...and dark...and there's no telling who, or what, you'll run into.

What you just might find out here in the deep dark East Texas woods is a friendly enough looking old guy who'll invite you to follow him even deeper into the darkness. He'll motion you to walk down a cleared pathway that cuts between the pines until you get to a certain spot. Then the friendly enough looking old guy will, in a very friendly way and with the biggest grin you've ever seen, show you his...dinosaurs.

That's right, dinosaurs. You wonder why some peculiar stories come out of the deep dark East Texas woods? This is why. There are big dinosaurs in them thar trees. And they all belong to a country boy who wanted to make a little money off his livestock. And he wasn't talking cattle.

"I don't know why I'm so enthused, " the friendly looking old guy tells us. "I just like dinosaurs, I like all of them. I sit and stare at them quite a bit. I still like to walk around these trails, as many times as I've done it, I go out there and look at them everyday and see how they're doing."

What you've got here is Dinosaur Gardens in

64

Moscow, Texas. It all started more than 30 years ago when Donald Bean and his wife and two kids took a station wagon trip into Oregon. They were driving along when all of a sudden out of nowhere there was this dinosaur park. That was all it took. Donald Bean had to have his own dinosaurs and his own dinosaur park.

"When I saw it I jumped on the brakes and pulled in to see it. It was great. From that moment on I planned to someday open my own place. Then I went back to see it again just before we opened our dinosaur park."

Donald Bean's Dinosaur Gardens. Going south on 59 you'll pass through Moscow and then you'll see it...a 30-foot tall welcome wagon grinning at you, one of eleven that live at the park. For less than lunch at the Dairy Queen you can pull in and see Donald's dream come true.

So, where does a guy get 30-foot tall dinosaurs? Donald found his up on the Red River. Seems he ran across a guy who builds those fiberglass bulls you see up on the roofs of steakhouses and he told Donald sure, he could build a dinosaur. The way he saw it they were just bigger, uglier and had more teeth. So now you can see things like Mr. Stegosaurus, the dinosaur with two brains.

"The brain in his head was only the size of a walnut," Donald tells us. "Some of the school kids that come through here call him Mr. Stupid, but he couldn't have been that stupid cause his kind survived over 150 million years."

Besides strolling through Dinosaur Gardens, Donald's got souvenirs to offer. Dinosaur toys and bone belt buckles, dinosaur books and, believe it or not, toothbrush holders. It's all part of Donald Bean's dinosaur dream.

"When I saw it I jumped on the brakes and pulled in to see it."
-Donald Bean

One of Donald Bean's dinosaurs.

You'll find Donald Bean's Dinosaur Gardens on Highway 59 south of Moscow, Texas, between Livingston and Corrigan near the intersection with Rt. 2. During the summer they're open seven days a week 'til sundown, after Labor Day they are open on weekends but you can make special arrangements to visit during the week. A tour will only cost you $2.50 if you're grown and $1.50 if you're only part-way grown. Anyone under 2 gets in free. 409-398-4565

Discover Nature's Hidden Beauty at the Johnson Rock Shop

Imagine finding a beautiful work of art -- something that has never been seen before. Something that has remained locked away and hidden for millions of years until the very moment you look upon it.

Ottis Johnson enjoys just such an experience almost every day. All it takes is a sharp saw and a keen eye for good rocks.

Stop #22
Livingston, TX

At the Johnson Rockshop in Livingston, Texas, Ottis Johnson has got hundreds of previously hidden treasures on display.

"You cut into a good stone, and there's a picture in there that's 80 million years old," Ottis says, "It's something no one on this earth has ever seen. It's like it was just sitting there waiting for you to discover it."

If you've ever stopped somewhere and you're not quite sure if you're in the right place, trust us...you will know when you have found the Johnson Rock Shop. The sign out front makes it perfectly clear. It reads,

There ain't no place anywhere around this place that looks anything like this place, so this must be the place.

Therefore, it could be, might be, must be, has to be, is definitely the best little rock shop in the piney woods.

The Johnson Rock Shop is really a collection of six home-made buildings that house Ottis' enormous rock collection. Each room has a different theme, its own unique design, its own personality depending on the type of rock.

Ottis started cutting and collecting rocks about 25 years ago. He had hurt himself bad in an accident and turned to rocks for a hobby. His

67

hobby grew into an obsession and the obsession grew into a business. Stop in and let Ottis show you around.

Most of the colorful rocks that surround Ottis' life formed from eons of hot lava and sand. But some were once trees -- driftwood that floated in on swollen rivers from another place and time and has somehow found its way into the Johnson Rock Shop.

Ottis Johnson, the all-time rock collector.

"Most of this wood is 75 to 80 million years old," Ottis boasts, "And I probably have the largest collection in the state of Texas right here in my backyard."

Now Ottis doesn't sell "pet" rocks, but he is quick to point out the advantages of having a nice pretty rock that won't chew on your shoes.

"You don't have to feed them or water them or worry about them staying around. And if they do disappear, maybe they'll do somebody good where they went. Maybe the next person will look at that rock, enjoy it and be a caretaker of it until the next person comes along."

Among the rocks you'll find in Ottis' shop are gypsum and quartz, agate and ore. Each piece an Ottis Johnson hand picked treasure. But as Ottis puts it, you won't find a single "Leaverite" in the place. ("Leaverite" -- that's rock talk for a bad stone that Ottis plans to *leave her right* where she's sitting, cause that rock ain't worth picking up.)

Take a afternoon and stroll though the Johnson Rock Shop. Ottis will tell you an earful about each and every rock. He's that kind of guy, Ottis. He'd just as soon sit out on the front porch and talk about rocks than sell you every one he's got.

The Johnson Rock Shop is on Wiggins Street in the Indian Springs Subdivision in Livingston, Texas. Just follow the signs. They are open seven days a week from 8am to 5pm, on Thursdays they are only open until 3. Call before you go to make sure someone is at the store, sometimes they have to close for a bit. 409-563-4438

"You don't have to feed them or water them or worry about them staying around. And if they do disappear, maybe they'll do somebody good where they went."
-Ottis Johnson

A Backwoods Tour of the Big Thicket

Stop #23
Kountz, TX

"There is plenty here that you see nowhere else. It is one of the most unique geographic areas of the country."
-*Doc Henry Hooks*

Whoever first called the thick, forested area of East Texas the "Big Thicket" did a good job naming this kaleidoscope of nature. At one time the Big Thicket was just that...a jungle barrier across East Texas, millions of acres of woodlands, marshes, rivers, streams and underbrush. Indian trails and the paths of wild animals were the only breaks in the thicket, and even the Indians did not stray too far off the pathways. You can scarcely see the sun here, even in the middle of the day.

The Big Thicket is one of the most unusual areas of Texas, and is one of the hardest to describe to someone who has not visited. It's a merging point of fauna and foliage, a crossroads of the country, where you can find an eastern hardwood growing next to desert cactus. Four out of the five insect-eating plants in the United States grow here. There is plant life here that is not found anywhere else.

The Big Thicket National Preserve was created by an act of congress in 1974. Eighty-six thousand acres were set aside in an effort to preserve the area. Today the thicket consists of an area bordered by U.S. 190 on the north side, U.S. 90 on the south, the Trinity River on the west and the Neches River on the east. Thousands of people visit the Big Thicket every year.

James and Nelda Overstreet have shed new light on the subject with a way to look into the thick of things. Through their Timber Ridge Tours you can get a good look at the place from a comfortable seat on their barge the Jayhawker. Float down the Neches River and you'll see the flora and fauna of the place and hear its story as told by natives to the area.

"This place is a phenomenon," Doc Henry Hooks, a Big Thicket native says. "There is plenty here that you see nowhere else.

For a small fee James and Nelda Overstreet will take you on a tour up and down the Neches River and into the Big Thicket. They are a part of this place and feel an obligation to share it with those who are "less fortunate."

To find out about Timber Ridge Tours you can call or stop by their office located at 200 Fox at the corner of Highway 59 in Kountz. If they are not there, the mailbox will be full of brochures. Costs vary according to the type of trip you want to take. Call 409-246-3107

The natural beauty of the Big Thicket.

Elissa - The Grand Lady of Galveston

Stop #24
Galveston, TX

"I must go down to the seas again, to the lonely sea and the sky. And all I ask is a tall ship and a star to steer her by."
- John Mansfield

We want you to come with us now to Galveston. If you've ever had dreams of sailing ships, of salty air and buccaneers, this is the place to be.

The year is 1883. Galveston, Texas. The Strand is in all its glory -- busy, rich and raucous. In the street are the scents of spices, in the air is the smell of the sea.

In the harbor sometimes as many as a hundred tall ships crowd in for the lucrative business here. You see, Texas is the king of cotton and Galveston is queen of the coast. Among the ships here is a barque out of Scotland named Elissa.

She is small by tall ship standards, but she is sleek and she makes a splendid living on the sea. When she last leaves Galveston in 1887, the wind is at her back and her fortunes are on the rise. It is a great time to be a sailing ship.

In the 1960s Elissa found herself one step from the scrapheap, abandoned in a Greek shipyard, with almost no trace of her past and little left for her future.

But the people of Galveston wanted Elissa back, so they went and got her.

Half a world away Galveston was getting a facelift. New energy was putting the old pizazz back in the Strand, and the tall ship Elissa was all that was missing.

They started work on Elissa in 1975. Folks in Galveston saw in Elissa a new icon for their city, a prize for the state of Texas.

Through hundreds of donations and thousands of hours of labor, craftspeople from across the country gathered in Galveston to make her again what she once was -- a grand sailing ship from the turn of the century.

The tall ship is the centerpiece of the Texas Seaport Museum, a waterfront tribute to bustling days of commerce along the Strand.

If you are interested in seeing Elissa, you can find her on Pier 21 in Galveston. In the summer you can see her 9:30am-5:30pm, in the winter her hours are 10am-5pm. Be sure to call the Galveston Historical Foundation for ticket and further information at 409/765-7834.

Elissa, the ship rescued from the scrap heap.

The George Observatory - Gateway to the Heavens

Brazos Bend State Park, only 45 miles south of the hustle and hubbub of Houston. Bordered on the banks of the Brazos River, the marshy edges of the park soak up the sites and sounds of the city like a sponge, leaving 5,000 acres of wild land and clean, clear air. It's a special place, a place you'd expect to find the rare and extraordinary. And you won't get much more extraordinary than this: deep in the thickets of Brazos Bend is a window to the universe.

Nat Shapiro was the first manager of the George Observatory, the state's newest gateway to the stars. Inside the main dome is a twelve ton, 36 inch telescope. In astronomy circles its a first class ticket to the heavens. That alone is rare. What's extraordinary is that you and your neighbors are invited to come along.

"Nowhere else in the United States is there a facility that has this to offer," Nat said, "that the amateur astronomer can come to. It's all here for them, and the price is right. It's free."

Used to be the closest we amateurs ever got to the stars was through the lens of a movie projector. Up there, on the wall in science class were galaxies and solar systems that only professional astronomers ever saw for real. Not any more. It cost over a million dollars, but Houston's George Foundation bought one of the biggest telescopes this side of NASA and built it a home in Brazos Bend where the skies are clear and the nights pitch dark. It was a remarkable project funded by donations and shepherded by volunteers.

Already thousands of anxious amateurs have asked for a chance to peek into space.

Currently, the observatory is open to the public Saturday nights, first come-first served, two dozens at a time every half hour. The biggest job these days is training the dozens of volunteers who pilot the giant telescopes across the heavens.

"Depending on what's good at that time of the year, " Nat explained, "we show them all kinds of different things. We show them nebula, we show them exploded stars, we show them planets, if Saturn is there with its rings, we show them just all kinds of things. The excitement of seeing something that is maybe millions of years old gives you a perspective of complete wonderment. The very idea that we're seeing something that 300 years ago wasn't seen by any man previous to that time, it's more excitement than you can measure. Very few people come away disappointed."

Deep in the dark thickets of Brazos Bend State Park, Nat Shapiro has seen a dream come true. The window is open and thousands of Texans come calling with stars in their eyes.

You can come calling, too. The trip to Brazos Bend State Park is well worth it without the observatory. With it, well, it's almost unbelievable.

Since we visited, Nat has moved on to other projects. Dana Lambert is carrying on in his place. Brazos Bend State Park and the George Observatory is off of FM 762. The observatory is open to the public on Saturdays from 3pm to 10pm in the winter, until 11pm in the summer. Programs and costs vary, so call for more information. 713-242-3055 or 409-553-3400

"The very idea that we're seeing something that 300 years ago wasn't seen by any man previous to that time, it's more excitement than you can measure. Very few people come away disappointed."
-Nat Shapiro

The Last Living Memorial to the Days When Cotton Was King

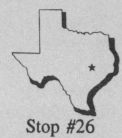

Stop #26
Burton, TX

"I came around the corner and it startled me...I couldn't believe this great engine was just sitting there."

-Doug Hutchinson

For more than a hundred years cotton was the major crop in Texas. It sustained entire towns. It made folks rich. Great engines from the cotton gins throbbed from dawn until long past dark and the air was rich with the smell of cotton seed. Then things changed, and cotton wasn't king anymore.

Like a lot of other cotton towns of the past, Burton, Texas, appears to be losing the battle against time and change. Were it not for one old relic left standing just off Main Street, this tiny town of about 300 might have disappeared all together. But the Burton Farmers Cotton Gin has kept hope alive.

Doug Hutchinson was a tourist who couldn't resist stopping in this small town with the same name as his hometown, Burton, Ohio. What he stumbled on by accident one afternoon changed his life, and changed the lives of the 300 or so people of Burton.

"I was out taking pictures and someone jokingly said I shouldn't miss the gin, so I took 'em serious," Doug says. "I came around the corner and it startled me...I couldn't believe this great engine was just sitting there. It was spooky. The gin looked like someone blew a whistle and everyone left for lunch."

What Doug had discovered wasn't just a cotton gin. It was history. Everything about the gin was intact right down to the bookkeeper's records of who ginned how much on which day. It was one of the last remaining complete cotton gins of that era in the nation.

Doug convinced the town of Burton the old gin was worth saving, so in 1986 Operation Restoration got underway.

Today you can see the history of cotton just by stopping by the Burton Farmers Cotton Gin. You can walk through the gin and see the evolution of cotton ginning from the hand-picked days right up to the machine-picked era. All the records are there from the day the gin was formed by the farmers. It's an historic treasure.

Burton Farmers Cotton Gin, history restored by the townsfolk.

They are so proud of the cotton gin in Burton, the mayor will even give you a guided tour, if you ask. And, if you'd like to visit on your own, they'll toss you the key and let you show yourself around.

And every year on the third weekend of April they throw a big shabang called the Burton Farmers Cotton Gin Festival. There's a Saturday morning parade, rides and games, arts and crafts and tours of the town and the gin. The population swells by a hundred times or so for that one weekend and it's a heckuva good time.

You can find the Burton Farmers Cotton Gin half way between Austin and Houston off Highway 290. Exit onto loop 125 and you will find yourself on Main Street in Burton. Stop and ask directions to the gin from there. Everyone in town knows where it is. When you get to the gin, go across the street to the General Store, get yourself a drink and let them know that you want to tour the gin. They will call someone to come over and give you a tour. Tours are available whenever you arrive. No fee is charged for a tour, however donations are accepted. For more information you can call the Chamber of Commerce at 409-289-3849.

The Stuermer Store--
A Warehouse of History,
A Place of the Past

Travel U.S. 290 between Austin and Brenham and you'll pass through a handful of little towns built before the days of chrome and glass. These are towns built by farmers who made a living earning what they could scratch out of the ground. They were people who traveled into town only when they needed to, dropping by the general mercantile to pick up "stores". They used everything until it was all used up and rarely threw anything away.

Stop #27
Ledbetter, TX

Chris Jervis and her mother Lillian have never thrown anything away...at least anything worth its weight in memories, and for over a century pieces of the past have piled up at the Stuermer Store. In a way Chris and Lillian have transformed the place from mercantile to museum.

"The store was in this spot in 1870," Chris tells us. "It was owned by several different people before 1890 when my great grandfather started his saloon business. The next year he bought the store which has been open and in operation by our family ever since."

A hundred plus years of continuous operation. The only time the store has ever closed is for an occasional illness or a funeral. Even when the surrounding town of Ledbetter began to disappear, the store remained. Lillian has lived a lifetime along the aisles.

"My brother and I, we had a few jobs around here back in the days when you had to pump the gas by hand," she says. "Our reward was soda water in the afternoon. And sometimes we got cheese and crackers."

In the past hundred years, time has swept

"Of course, times are changing and so what the next few years holds we don't have any way of knowing."
-Mother Lillian

79

through Ledbetter but somehow missed the Stuermer Store. These days they put the old stuff on display for anybody who has an interest to see.

Today the Stuermer Store stands as a warehouse of history, a place of the past holding its own in a tiny speck of a town. Take a look inside and you'll find more than ten decades of memories and a family

Chris Jervis, shopkeeper at the Stuermer Store.

determined to keep things the way they used to be...the way they've always been at the Stuermer Store. But who knows what the future holds for places like this?

"Of course, times are changing and so what the next few years holds we don't have any way of knowing. I think some of the grandchildren have sort of said they'll keep it going, but you never can tell what will happen," Mother Lillian says.

For now, though, the doors are still open at the Stuermer Store. And you can still drop by and see a piece of the old days. Better hurry.

You can find the Stuermer Store at the intersection of Highway 290 and FM 1291. If you're headed to Houston or Austin, the Stuermer Store is a perfect place to stretch your legs, have a soft drink and visit with Chris. They are open Monday through Saturday 7am to 5:30pm. 409-249-5642

A hundred-year-old family heirloom.

The Whoopers --
A Rare Encounter
With a Rare Texas Guest

Stop #28
Rockport, TX

"A few guys having a few good meals and making money off the sale of feathers almost cost us an entire species."
-*A Whooping Crane tour guide*

By the time you can see the sun in Rockport, most of the fishing boats have already left the harbor. But aboard one heavy, sea-worn vessel things are a little different. There are no fishing reels, cut bait or casting rods aboard The Wharf Cat. The boat slowly glides out to the open bay with one thing in common among those making the trip: a patient desire to witness one of the most dramatic comeback stories in Texas history.

What the folks on board the Wharf Cat are hoping for is to catch a glimpse of one of the rarest birds in North America. It is a tall, proud bird which nests in northwest Canada, then migrates to Texas to the brackish waters of the Aransas National Wildlife Refuge to spend the winter with other, similar birds like the Great Blue Herron. What the folks on board the Wharf Cat are hoping for is to catch a glimpse of a whooping crane.

As the Wharf Cat continues its journey through the marshlands, the folks on board are anxious for a glimpse of maybe even one whooping crane, keeping in mind there are only about 200 in the entire world. A look at one will require patience, a little luck and a love for a graceful creature that we almost lost forever.

"They were almost extinct," one guide says. "A few people hunting these beautiful birds and collecting their feathers to make hats did that. A few guys having a few good meals and making money off the sale of feathers almost cost us an entire species."

While the guide continues his story of how

pollution and poaching almost killed all the whoopers, the crowd spots something off the starboard bow. It is two survivors calmly feeding a pair of whooping cranes, healthy and content.

"It is such a thrill to see something that has survived a real perilous time in their history," one bird watcher says. "And there they are, standing there so beautiful and serene after such a terrible time they've been through. It

Whooping cranes, a sight to cherish.

reminds me of freedom and that we have an obligation to the other things in this world besides ourselves."

On this day, the Wharf Cat is filled with birdwatchers and biologists, amateurs and professionals who have one thing in common. Each and every person on board believes in their heart that there is, and always should be, room in this world for a tall, white, graceful bird called the whooping crane. While the two cranes jab the salty mud for breakfast, a symbol of hope appears through the marsh grass. A family of three whoopers stand proud against the horizon as if to say "Look at us! We made it!"

The sight brings tears to the eyes of several passengers.

Sightings of whooping cranes are usually brief and at a distance. That's the way the whoopers want it. Past encounters with man have almost killed them. These days, folks like those on board the Wharf Cat are trying to make amends.

There are several boat trips out of Rockport to see the whooping cranes. Should anyone tell you they'll get you an up close and personal look at the birds, don't go. That's not the idea behind these visits. We are merely visitors to their world and up close and personal is an intrusion.

Rockport is located north of Aransas Pass and south of Fulton. RR881 will take you right into town. You might try Captain Ted's Whooping Crane Tour, we've been on that one a couple of times, too. 512-729-9589

The South Padre Sand Castle Man - a Son of The Beach

Some of us never grow up. And what's wrong with that? There are plenty of adults and adult attitudes in this world. Not that we should all run screaming through the aisles at the grocery store or cry when it's time for bed or ride skateboards through the mall, but a little childlike view of the world around us isn't a bad thing. Too bad most folks seem to have lost that.

Stop #29
South Padre, TX

We know a guy, though, who refuses to grow up. And he's managed to make a living out of it.

Walter McDonald remembers his childhood and all the fun things you get to do when you're a kid. Things like taking the summer off, going barefoot in public, wearing goofy clothes and building sand castles on the beach. Today Walter McDonald still does all that stuff and has even more fun than he did when he was a kid. That's because Walter McDonald is better known as the Amazing Walter, professional sand castle builder.

Now most of you are probably saying "what kind of job is that?" And the rest of you are saying "where can I apply?" But the Amazing Walter is no mere beach bum. He's an artist.

"It is art," the Amazing tells us. "Temporary art, but art. These things take time and, yes, talent. Anyone can build a sand castle, but we've developed sand castle construction to a higher level."

One thing about being a sand castle artist...the art supplies are cheap.

"It's just sand and water," Amazing says. "And there is an unlimited supply to be found

85

right at the location where you want to do your building. And it's all free!"

The Amazing Walter practices his art on South Padre Island. And he's not alone. Walter has a sidekick named Sandy Feet and they've been playing in the sand together for years. They call their sand castle construction company Sons of the Beach. The Sons of the Beach build 'em, the waves of the beach

Amazin' Walter and Sandy Feet at work.

wash 'em away. It's kind of a frustrating proposition, but Walter doesn't see it that way.

"Why does something have to be permanent to be enjoyed," he asks. "That's just not the way life is. This should truly be a lesson in living for the moment, enjoying the here and now *here and now* instead of always looking forward to tomorrow. Not that we shouldn't plan ahead, but not always at the expense of today. If you know something you like will not be here in the morning, you'll appreciate it's beauty even more while you can."

Walter and Sandy don't just build sand castles for their own amusement. They are entertainers, singing and juggling while they create elaborate castles on the beach. And they do all this with a message: don't litter. Make that "unlitter". In other words, Walter and Sandy don't just want you not to throw your trash on the Texas beaches, they want you to help get rid of what's already there. There is even an official unlitter newsletter published by the Sons of the Beach. These beach bums aren't just bums.

"These things take time and, yes, talent. Anyone can build a sand castle, but we've developed sand castle construction to a higher level."
-Amazing Walter

"Our Texas beaches are wonderful places," Walter says. "But we're destroying them with our garbage. If we visit, we should not only leave the place as clean as we found it, we should leave it cleaner."

You can find The Amazing Walter and Sandy Feet, The Sons of the Beach, behind the hotels in the town of South Padre. All they ask for their entertainment is that you take some garbage with you when you go. They will even give you sandcastle construction lessons for $25. 210-761-6222

Gruene, Texas and The State's Oldest Honky Tonk

Stop #30
New Braunfels, TX

"We just happened through at the right time and had the guts to take a chance on the place."
-Pat Molak

Cross over the Guadalupe River on the northern edge of New Braunfels, head up through the golden dappled oaks and hackberries and twist and wind your way down the lonely backroads leading to Gruene, Texas.

Now before we go any further, let's get it straight -- you pronounce it: "Green". Honest.

Gruene is nothing more than an intersection of Gruene and Hunter Streets just north of New Braunfels -- two streets and a half a dozen hundred-year-old buildings named after a wealthy cotton plantation family who settled the place.

You could say that back then, back when cotton was king and a good crop made you a wealthy man, that this tiny crossroads was the Gruene dream. Crops were ginned at the family mill and farmhands traded at the family store. It was a busy place for a while. Then things went bad. The dream didn't work anymore and the tiny town of Gruene was all but a wisp of a cobweb on some old forgotten roadmap.

For 40 years after the depression hit and cotton died, the once bustling buildings here did little more than whistle in the wind. The founding Gruene family even gave up on the place. Today old Frank Schlather is about the only one left to tell what things were like.

"Cotton went out and it was nothing but a beer joint," Frank remembers. "Seemed like almost overnight this placed died."

Yep, old Frank remembers. He remembers Gruene as a ghost town most of his life, weathering in the sun and rustling in the rain.

Then the strangers came and turned this place around.

Pat Molak was one of the strangers to Gruene. He was an unhappy stockbroker from San Antonio looking for a way out. In 1974, he and some partners heard about a ghost town by the Guadalupe that was about to be bulldozed for riverfront condos. Pat and his friends stopped by for a look and they've been here ever since.

Pat Molak two steppin' in Gruene Hall.

Little by little, Pat Molak and company fixed this old town up, and little by little the tourists trickled in. The old H.D. Gruene Mercantile became an antique store. Out back is a pottery. Even the tumbled Gruene gristmill has been converted into a restaurant, and the decrepit Gruene mansion has been restored as a family inn. The once forgotten cavernous Gruene Hall

89

is now a legendary Texas honky tonk. In fact, a few years ago, Jerry Jeff Walker recorded an album here complete with the usual Gruene Hall hoopin' and hollerin'.

On a good Saturday night, they pack the place shoulder to shoulder. There's longneck beer, and Texas tunes, lots of cowboys and big-haired women. Even if you don't drink and can't dance, it's still a great place to get away from it all.

It's that kind of place Gruene, where every weekend is sort of a celebration -- a backroads bash toasting the realization of Pat Molak's dream.

"If we hadn't come through we'd be standing in a townhouse right now," Pat says. "We just happened through at the right time and had the guts to take a chance on the place. It's like my child now. I couldn't be more proud."

The sun has come up on Gruene, Texas again. New paint, new business, new life. Today Gruene is one of our favorite weekend retreats, we hope to see you there.

To get to Gruene take FM 306 northwest off of I-35 near New Braunfels, and drive a mile and a half to Hunter road. Turn left and head into Gruene where you can find the visitors center at 1601 Hunter Road. There you can arrange tours and ask questions. They are open Monday through Friday 8am to 5pm. 210-629-5077

The Cave Without a Name

One thing we've learned in our travels is that Texans are resourceful. We're good at making do with what we have -- making a living and getting by playing the hand we're dealt.

Down in Boerne, Texas, we found a man making a decent living selling tours of a hole in the ground, and just about any time you can drop by for a personal tour. Eugene Ebell owns a cave.

As far as we know there's not another cave in the state quite like this. See, Eugene lives right above this magnificent cavern. His house serves as the office, his porch is the waiting area, and the cave entrance is right there in the front yard. If he's not around have a seat on the porch step and he'll be back in a few minutes.

Down a dim stairway and into the cool, damp, darkness, you follow behind Eugene and listen to his thick German accent and his explanation of stalagmites and stalactites and underground rivers.

From the surface you would never guess that Eugene Ebell owns one of the largest and most beautiful caves in the hill country.

"I've had all kinds of geologists and professors down here with all kinds of letters behind their names, and I ask them why this cave is so big," Eugene says. " They just shake their heads, they can't explain it."

Now you have to wonder what a place of such grandeur would be called. After racking his brain for years to decide what to call his cave, a little boy suggested Eugene call it "The Cave Without a Name". So he did and the name stuck. The Cave Without a Name has had a name ever since.

For nearly thirty years Eugene has been taking people on tours through his cave. He

Stop #31
Boerne, TX

"This place is one-of-a-kind. This is Texas. This is what you call being deep in the heart of Texas."
-Eugene Ebell

estimates he's been down there more than twenty-five thousand times, and ever time he sees something new.

But one thing you won't see here is an amusement park on top or fancy commercials and billboards to bring people in. Eugene says his cave speaks for itself.

"Everything you need to see is down here. I don't need a lot of Ballyhoo going on up there."

You can find The Cave Without a Name on State Highway 474 about thirteen miles outside of Boerne. It's certainly worth the trip. Like Eugene says, "People make trips to Paris, Rome or London because they are one-of-a-kind. This place is one-of-a-kind. This is Texas. This is what you call being deep in the heart of Texas."

Eugene will be happy to give you a tour for just $5 for adults and $2 if you're a youngster. He is open from 9:30am to 4:30pm Monday, Wednesday, Thursday and Friday.   210-537-4212

Eugene Ebell, owner of the Cave Without a Name.

The Old West Museum-- Shooting Down the Cowboy Myth

Okay, you already know about the Alamo, Six Flags Over Texas, and all the state parks. You can get volumes of information on all the water parks, Sea World and every lake in the state. And, if it's a museum you want, there are lots of those, too, with fancy brochures and traveling exhibits. But there's one place you probably won't find on some who's who list of the state's fancy attractions: Gish's Old West Museum.

Stop #32
Fredericksburg, TX

Joe Gish has never been a cowboy. He wasn't born on a ranch and he's not even from the west. He was raised on a farm in Kansas, but Joe has a thing about the old west, about cowboys, six shooters and saddlebags. He collected so much of the stuff, there was only one thing to do. He opened his own Gish's Old West Museum.

The old outlaw and lawman gun leather and guns is Joe's favorite part of the collection. He has a Colt 45 found in the dirt in Utah with two chambers still loaded. "If only this weapon could talk," Joe says. He has belts and holsters and guns and badges and hats and anything from the old west. And not one item in the museum is a recreation. It's living history, every item was actually used or worn by someone in the old west. Every piece has a story and tells a story.

"The way Hollywood portrays those folks is purely romantic. It's just not the way it was."
-Joe Gish

Joe Gish's museum actually started as a prop collection. Joe liked to paint pictures of things from the old west, but he needed to see it to draw it. Before long he had more stuff than he knew what to do with, so he built it a little house of its own, hung a shingle out front and invited passersbys to come in for a visit.

"Actually, the time most people refer to as the old west was a short period, from just after the Civil War until 1890 or so," Joe explains. "Then it died out pretty quickly."

But at Joe Gish's place, the old west lives on. So do cowboys. He likes them and all their stuff. In fact, he can't seem to get enough of it. Just when he thinks he has all he can ever admire, all he can ever put on display, Joe runs across something else, another piece of western memorabilia. Before long, it's displayed in Gish's Old West Museum.

"I'm fascinated with the era," Joe tells us. "And I want people to know the real story behind the time and its people. The way Hollywood portrays those folks is purely romantic. It's just not the way it was."

Gish's Old West Museum is located at 502 North Milam Street in Fredericksburg. Take Main Street heading west and turn right on North Milam. There is no charge to see the museum, and it is "open when I'm here," Joe says. You can call ahead to make sure he's around. While you're in town you might want to stop by one of the little German bakeries up on Main Street and look around some of the stores or even take a run down to Enchanted Rock. Joe will be back. He's too eager to tell you about the old west to stay gone long. 210-997-2794

Westcave Preserve -
"This Can't Be Texas"

By now, we're pretty accustomed to the signs of progress. We expect to encounter construction wherever we go. Traveling the backroads as we do, we have grown used to seeing new building of homes and highways where there once were fields and prairies and forests. When this traveling job began in the early 70s, there were more wide open spaces than we see today. In that short amount of time, we have gobbled up the open land to make room for more of us and to create our creature comforts.

I do know of one spot that probably looks pretty much the same as it always has. It's in an area called Cypress Mill, not too far outside of Austin. Just off the Pedernales (pronounced perd-nal-is) River is a place we call "mother nature's living room", Westcave Preserve. It's a complete ecological system without interference from man. It looks like it looked to our forefathers.

"We've gone throughout Texas and changed it," John Ahrns says. John is the keeper of Westcave. "We've taken out this or added that because it didn't suit us. We've changed the course of rivers, we've relocated animal and plant species and we've built on top of it all. And when you change the way the system is naturally, the way it was meant to be, the system starts to fall apart."

John watches over this spot on the Edwards Plateau where two ecosystems collide, creating a living museum of contrast and color. It's an ecological wonderland virtually untouched by human hand. It is as it was.

What you'll see at Westcave Preserve is a

Stop #33
Cypress Mill, TX

95

dense forest growing around a clear stream which pours from the rocks that form a small cave. There is a tiny trail leading down a hillside through the trees, the only acknowledgement of man's existence. It is a complex web of more than 400 species of plants alone. It is a special niche that somehow has survived. It almost did not. Ironically, the generation that claimed to be trying to save the

John Ahrns at Westcave Preserve

planet did the most harm to Westcave. During the 60s and 70s, the cave was a popular party spot for the flower children. When John Ahrns arrived, he found Westcave littered with beer bottles and such. It was almost destroyed.

"I picked up over a hundred sacks of trash from the area around the pool alone," John says. "We caught it in the nick of time. Hopefully, I saw it at its all time low and it's been uphill since. I'm just glad this is what it ended up being."

There are so few places left that have not been changed by our culture that we hesitate to even mention Westcave for fear of causing it's demise. Too many people and too much society and Westcave could easily look like an amusement park version of itself. In other words, it really needs to be left alone. But then, we couldn't learn from it if we couldn't see it. John Ahrns says Westcave is to nature what the animals in the zoo are to their relatives left in the wild...ambassadors to mankind, in hopes that man *is* kind.

You can visit Westcave, but we plead with you: no weddings, no company picnics. Take a small group and take a look. Then get out. And take nothing away with you except a few photographs and the knowledge of how things should be, how they could be.

The Westcave Preserve is open for tours on Saturdays and Sundays. Tours are at 10am, 12pm, 2pm and 4pm. During the week group tours are scheduled. They are open year-round, weather permitting. To get there follow Highway 71 west of Austin to Village Bee Cave. Take a left on RR3238(Hamilton Pool Rd), go 14 miles, cross the river and it's your first gate on the right. Reservations are not required and tours are free but donations are accepted. 210-825-3442

"I picked up over a hundred sacks of trash from the area around the pool alone... we caught it in the nick of time."
-John Ahrns

Vanishing Texas
River Cruise

Stop #34
Burnet, TX

Much of the beauty of Texas jumps right out at you. You can even see it while driving down the interstate, so you know it's got to have a strong will to survive there. Bluebonnets and Indian Paintbrush growing on the side of the road, thick forests spreading right up to the blacktop, hawks perched on telephone polls.

But much of the beauty of Texas is hidden. It's elusive and to see it you have to work for it, searching the depths of the wilderness to catch even a fleeting glimpse of some rare flora or fauna. That is the mission of the Vanishing Texas River Cruise.

Come with us now to the Colorado River, to the northern edge of Lake Buchanan. It is the first week of November, eagle time in these parts. This is where the American Bald Eagle likes to spend its winters. From just before first frost until just before that moment when you first feel a hint of spring in the air, the symbol of America makes an appearance in Texas to avoid the cold weather of Canada at that time of year. The birds usually choose an area that's not too crowded, especially with human types, where there's plenty of fishing and lots of cover. The best area for that runs through some private ranch land up the Colorado River from Lake Buchanan. Were it not for the fact that the waterway that runs through the privately held acreage belongs to the State of Texas, we would not have an opportunity to view the eagles.

The "Eagle II" is a specially built boat that carries a hundred or so passengers on a two and a half to three hour trip up the Colorado.

On the 25 mile round trip, visitors are treated to wildlife, wildflowers and scenic areas like no other, certainly not like those you can see from the interstate. In fact, you'd be hard pressed to find anything like this this close to civilization. Austin is a mere 75 miles away, yet this trip reveals an Ansel Adams photograph, a Thomas Cole painting of scenes most people only get to see in books and movies.

The "Eagle II" cruises the Colorado River.

For now, though, they are here. You can hop on board for a small fee and leave your big city ways and worries behind. Breathe in the sights and sounds of the wilderness. This is nature almost untouched, the way it used to be. On your journey you'll see hawks and herons and wild goats and big buck. You'll pass by a waterfall and rocky cliffs and caves. You will marvel at the beauty of the world.

99

The moment everyone awaits, however, is when the great, proud eagle graces us with his appearance. Everything else is just a warm-up act once the big bird arrives. The crowd ooohs and ahhhhhs, shutters snap away and some folks even cry.

When we first started traveling the backroads of Texas, there were only about 3,000 bald eagles left in the United States. Today, there are more than 20,000 and 500 of those call Texas home for a few months each year. You can visit them by means of the Vanishing Texas River Cruise.

To get to the Vanishing Texas River Cruise, from Burnett you drive 3 miles west on Highway 29 and then 13 miles north on RM 2341. Reservations are a must. The tour runs everyday except on Tuesdays from 11am to 1:30pm. On Saturdays May through October they offer a dinner cruise. The tour cost is $12.95 for adults, $11.50 for seniors, students, and active military, $8.95 for children and kids 5 years and younger are free. 512-756-6986

"On the 25 mile round trip, visitors are treated to wildlife, wildflowers and scenic areas like no other."

The Grove:
The Town That Time
Forgot

I can't tell you how many times over the years we've heard it. People of all kinds, all ages, all professions and from all areas of the state have told us. It's gotten to be a cliché. And I always wonder who said it first and if everyone else has just been copying that person or if they're all original thoughts and its just a coincidence. The phrase we've heard so often? "I guess I was born a hundred years too late."

Stop #35
The Grove, TX

Now the first time someone said that to us must have been when we first started traveling the backroads and talking to people about their lives, their hopes, their dreams and Texas...probably about 1972. Since then dozens, no, hundreds of people have said it. But the real reason we're telling you all this is because we really do know someone who was born too late. I'm not sure if it was a hundred years or just fifty or so, but I am sure that our friend Moody Anderson was born too late.

Moody is a junkaholic. Now we've met our share of them over the years, people who keep everything they've ever had and try to collect everyone else's share, too. People like Moody Anderson actually travel around looking for junk, only they don't think of it in those terms, and, to be fair, we shouldn't think of it in those terms either. Moody collects some pretty neat junk. But the neatest old junk Moody Anderson ever collected was The Grove.

That's right, The Grove, with a capital T and capital G. It's the name of a central Texas town. The Grove, Texas, population, well, just a few. It's one little piece of a street with a few buildings on it and our friend Moody

101

Anderson owns the whole thing, lock, stock and barrel. And there are plenty of locks, stocks and barrels of all kinds in The Grove.

In his <u>real</u> life you might say Moody is an antique dealer, or a junk dealer, depending on your outlook. But the one old thing Moody acquired that he couldn't part with is The Grove. Moody is mayor of his town. He's also the town's garbage collector. And the tax assessor. And the dog catcher. He is everything except the postmaster and that's only because the U.S. Postal service likes to choose that person themselves.

> *"It's one little piece of a street with a few buildings on it and our friend Moody Anderson owns the whole thing, lock, stock and barrel."*

Besides a post office, The Grove, Texas, is home to the W.J. Dube General Merchandise Store, the Cuckelbur Saloon, the Village Blacksmith Shop, a few other used-to-be businesses and the houses of the folks who call The Grove home. It's like stepping back in time (another cliché) when you pull into Moody Anderson's town. Everything is like it used to be, like it still is, in The Grove, Texas.

One thing for sure: Moody Anderson was born too late. But he found a remedy for that...he bought his own town and now he spends time in the era he likes best. You can too.

The Grove, Texas, can be found on the south side of Highway 36 at the intersection of Highway 236, just southeast of Gatesville, southwest of Waco. Tours are available on Saturdays and Sundays from 9am until 6pm. Admission is $2 for everyone. During the week you can reach Moody Anderson at 512-282-1215.

A Tiny Church That's Home to a Hermit

Fabian Raul Rosetti's closest neighbor is more than a mile away. Beyond that, for stretches in any direction, people are scarce as rain. Fabian Raul Rosetti wouldn't have it any other way. Completely alone on his hundred acre spread, in a valley near Christoval, Texas, Fabian Raul Rosetti is a hermit.

"I just came from being a pastor in a church," he said. "I finally realized that I needed to give up all material things and become a hermit."

He sings and chants the exact same words, at the exact same times, every day. He follows a schedule and does not have to impress anyone. He does not have to climb the corporate ladder. He has no money, no possessions and is completely unencumbered by worldly goods.

Father Fabian's tiny church is almost always empty. But he'll deliver the same prayer service three times a day at 6 in the morning, noon and 6 in the evening. There is no congregation and rarely a visitor. His only contact with people is when someone needs his help.

There is no television, no radio, no air conditioning. Just a vegetable garden and a few milk goats. Father Fabian lives by rules that are more than 700 years old, drawn up by a group of hermits who wanted to create guidelines for being a hermit in 13th century Europe. Those rules: stay simple, stay poor and give your time to prayer, but, most of all, give yourself to those in need.

Now there's one thing you have to understand about hermits. They can't fit into our life and still be hermits. The first thing some people will want to do is take Father Fabian a

Stop #36
Christoval, TX

"I live a very simple life without material needs so that I can go straight to my heart."
-Father Rosetti

television and a Hungerbuster. Don't do it. Father Fabian <u>chooses</u> to live the life he lives because, for him, it's the right thing to do. We admit, putting Father Fabian on television <u>did</u> change his life some. More and more folks are stopping by these days, but, please, don't stop just to gawk. What you <u>can</u> do, however, is call on Father Fabian when you have a problem. That's what he's there for. But

Father Fabian Rosetti, the Christoval hermit.

understand that he's not a prophet, not a miracle worker, and doesn't claim to be anything supernatural. He's a hermit and his job is to listen to your problems and pray for you. If you think that might help, go for it.

There is mass every day at 6:30am and at 10am on Sundays. You can go by 7 days a week from 6am to 6pm. From I10 exit

Highway 277 toward San Angelo. Christoval is about 15 miles south of San Angelo. Stop at Tony's Cafe. There you can get a bite to eat and directions to Father Rosetti. If you want to stay for a while, the hermitage has guest rooms available. You **must** write ahead of time to make reservations for a room. There is also a small bakery and gift shop. PO Box 337, Christoval, TX 76935-0337

Father Rosetti during a peaceful walk in the woods.

The Mysterious
Paint Rock Pictographs

Stop #37
Paint Rock, TX

The official population of Paint Rock, Texas, is 256, but that was years ago. Today folks around here say you would be lucky to find half that many. The streets of Paint Rock are for the most part empty. Main Street has slowly become a dusty old memory of a town.

No, Paint Rock is not the tourism capital of Texas, but it is certainly a tourist stop -- and being the accidental professional tourists we are, we couldn't pass up the simple sign that read, "Paint Rock Excursions."

A Paint Rock Excursion is a short trip up the scenic Concho River to a legendary place that folks around here have known about and kept to themselves for years. It's a very old, very special place that sits right in the middle of Kay Campbell's land. It's a place that only recently she's opened up to the public.

What the Campbells have been holding close like a treasured jewel is a place along a limestone bluff where prehistoric peoples painted hundreds of images that to this day modern man does not understand.

It's an eerie place where you can let your imagination run wild traveling back thousands of years of human history. Even the experts can't agree on who painted the pictographs -- or why.

Stroll along the bluff and the images from another time seem to taunt you with their knowledge of what has happened here in this place.

There are animal and human forms, plants, and symbols for the elements -- earth, water, fire, sun and moon. Most have not been precisely dated, but the pictures range in age from thousands to a few hundred years.

Equally fascinating is the number of pictographs. No one is sure why so many paintings are here in this one place. In all there are more than 1500. They are the primitive marking left by people who roamed the prairie centuries before Columbus landed in America.

"This will always be a mystery," Kay says. "These people were trying to say something. This was their attempt to communicate. We don't understand it, but these pictures tell us what happened here."

"Everybody would like to read letters their grandparents wrote. Well, this is a letter from the Indians to us."

Kay explains, "I always say it's kind of like having an elephant in your bathtub. You just can't ignore it."

The whole Paint Rock Excursion will take you about an hour and a half, and the footpath leading to the pictographs takes you within about 20 feet of the bluff. The office is located on U.S. highway 83 in downtown Paint Rock across from the courthouse. Making an appointment is the best way to do it but you can stop by if it's on your way. The tour costs $6 for adults, and $3 for children. Pre-schoolers are free. 915-732-4376

"This will always be a mystery...We don't understand it, but these pictures tell us what happened here."
-Kay Campbell

When it Comes to Making Saddles, Rector is the Real Story

Stop #38

San Angelo, TX

Ask just about any cowboy out San Angelo way where you can get help for a broken horn or a stitch in a busted stirrup, and any real cowboy worth his salt will tell you to go see Rector.

Yep, if you've got a sick saddle, need a shiny new one, or you just want to watch a master craftsman at work, drop by R.E. Donaho Concho Saddles in San Angelo and ask for Rector Story.

For more than a century, cowboys and ranchers all over the country have known that Concho Saddles are the best they can find, and for fifty of the past hundred years, Rector Story has been here patiently and quietly making saddles that have come to be known as the best saddles anywhere.

Rector owns the place even though the sign out front still displays another man's name. Back in 1938, when R.E. Donaho gave Rector a job as an apprentice saddle maker, neither man ever dreamed the teacher would some day sell the shop to the student. Nor did Mr. Donaho have any idea that more than fifty years later, his modest apprentice would still own the saddle shop and it would still bear the name of the man who hired him.

"Once a salesman came in here and said, 'I'd change that name if I were you', and I said, 'No, Donaho's been here a long time, and I'm not proud enough to have my name out front.'" If he did decide to change the name, though, he would probably change it to *Rector Story's Saddle School*. Seems most of the really fine saddle makers learned their trade in the backroom at Donaho's.

Concho Street used to be one of the most rootin' tootin' wild and wooly streets in the state of Texas, and the Donaho Saddle Shop sat stoically in the middle of it all -- brothels and bars from one end to the other.

Now you might think that in this day and age there's not much call for a saddle maker anymore. Fact is, Rector has all the business he can handle, especially when a new saddle is only a phone call away. Folks call from all over the U.S. and Canada to place an order. Some customers Rector's never even met.

There are other saddle shops, but few turn out the quality of a Donaho saddle. More and more these days, factories and machines are replacing the hand-made personal touch of a seasoned saddle maker. It's a trade that takes years to learn and years to teach -- time new apprentices aren't willing to spend.

"The young people want to work six months and be the boss," Rector remarks. "They go to these saddle making schools, build two or three saddles and they come out thinking they are a saddle maker. Really, they couldn't even repair in my shop without help."

The Donaho Saddle Shop is located at 8 E. Concho Street in downtown San Angelo. He is open for business 8am to 5:30pm Monday through Saturday (on Saturday they are closed for lunch.) 915-655-3270

"When I went to work here, it was about the wildest and roughest place you've ever seen in your life."
-Rector Story

San Angelo's 3rd of July: An Independent Celebration of Independence

Stop #39
San Angelo, TX

Small towns are just different. I can't really explain why, they just are. People in small towns look at things in a different way. They know one another and <u>talk</u> to one another. They know how to pull together and get things done because they have to. They're...well, they're just different.

San Angelo isn't what we call a small town. It's really a "small to medium", by our standards. Still, it has a lot of those small town characteristics. It's a place where lots of folks have known one another all their lives. They grew up together, found a way to stay on, marry, have children and grow old in the same place. People in San Angelo talk to one another and they get things done. Try <u>that</u> in the big city.

For instance, in San Angelo they don't even celebrate <u>freedom</u> in the same way as the rest of us. While all of America is doing the hot dogs and fireworks thing on the 4th of July, folks in San Angelo have already moved on to planning for Labor Day. See, in San Angelo, they don't celebrate the 4th of July on the 4th of July. They celebrate the 4th of July on the 3rd. Why? Simple, really. You know those big military cannons they shoot off at just about every Independence Day celebration in the USA? Well, the ones at the local armory are booked years in advance to another town, so folks in San Angelo just moved their party up a day. That's the way they get things done in small towns.

The annual celebration of freedom is such a big deal in San Angelo that almost everybody in town gets involved. Even mild mannered Ken Landon gets in on the fun. Ken is a botanist by trade...a pyrotechnician at heart. Ken is in charge of the local fireworks show.

"Fireworks in Japanese means 'flower fire'," he tells us. "And it really is fire in the shape of flowers, so I'm not that far out of my field."

Now most fireworks shows are conducted by professionals hired to do the job. But that would be too simple for the folks in San Angelo and not nearly enough fun. Ken teaches townsfolk how to assemble the rockets and where to put the fuses. It's a family affair, and its one heck of a 4th of July on the 3rd of July fireworks show.

But the celebration is more than just fireworks. Those who don't get into pyrotechnics might be members of the symphony orchestra. Gene Smith is the symphony conductor. He says the San Angelo celebration is much more than that. It's a matter of community pride where everybody comes together for one common purpose. It's not a fireworks show, not a symphony performance, it's a happening--small town Texas style.

"When you mix three very powerful ingredients together," he says, "the crowd of people gathered in a beautiful setting mixed with the patriotic music and the fireworks, it becomes an overwhelming experience for each individual."

For all the time and energy that goes into the San Angelo 3rd of July Show, most of the people there never get to see the fruits of their labor. The symphony orchestra must play to the crowd, so their backs are to the fireworks. And the fireworks volunteers are much too

"...the crowd of people gathered in a beautiful setting mixed with the patriotic music and the fireworks, it becomes an overwhelming experience for each individual."
-Gene Smith

busy on the ground to watch the sky. That's where you come in. They go to all this trouble every year for you. They put on this incredible show so you, the folks who aren't lucky enough to live in San Angelo, will come and enjoy the celebration. Maybe then you'll understand that small towns are different somehow. They talk to each other and get things done. They cooperate. They pull together.

To visit the San Angelo Independence Day Celebration, call 915-658-5877 to make reservations to ensure your seat at the celebration. The festivites are free, taking place at the San Angelo RiverStage located on the Concho river between Chadbourne and Oakes Streets. Entertainment begins at 6pm, concert at 8:45pm. F15 fighter jets are the most recent addition to the celebration. Believe me, you don't want to miss this!

Opal Hunt's Shrine to a Simpler Way of Life

After you have traveled as many miles as we have, you begin to notice certain rules of the road. No, not speed limits or things like that, but unwritten rules like -- The Texas Country Backroads Theorem #5: "When you've been somewhere too long, and you need to get somewhere else in a hurry, the backroads traveler will always see something of sufficient interest along the way requiring an investigatory stop."

Stop #40
Bradshaw, TX

We were only an hour behind schedule and about to roar through Bradshaw, Texas, when it happened. We saw it, we couldn't ignore it, and Theorem #5 had been proven true again. Bradshaw, Texas -- where a woman named Opal turned a family grocery store into a family museum.

It's the only grocery store in Bradshaw. In fact, it's about the *only* thing in Bradshaw. Opal Hunt's father opened the place for business back in 1905, and for years kept folks knee-high in dry goods and groceries. Things have changed.

Now at first you might think Opal is about the worst merchant in the state. I mean, the store's shelves are fully stocked, but nothing here's for sale.

"No, none of this is for sale." Opal says. "Not a thing in the whole place except soda pop."

Grab a soda pop and take a tour of Opal Hunt's life. Tucked away in this cavernous building with a sagging ceiling and a creaky old floor, you'll find a treasure trove of Hunt family heirlooms --a cookstove that was her mother's, the family's antique quilts, tables and

"This is all a part of me. These are my things and my family's things. I'm just as proud of this stuff as I can be."
-Opal Hunt

chairs and register receipts eight decades old.

What Opal Hunt has done here is preserve a frozen moment in Bradshaw's history. Oh, there's one other thing you'll find alongside the boxes of forty-year-old Washo Soap -- memories.

"This is all a part of me. These are my things and my family's things. I believe in life, but if you don't have a past, then you don't have a present or a future. I'm just as proud of this stuff as I can be," Opal says.

Opal Hunt represents something we've lost. She is a throwback to a time when family meant more than it does to most of us today. Folks back then didn't have much else but family, so you could be sure that, for the most part, they were going to protect what they had. Opal takes it a step further. She's holding on to what once was, a kind of shrine to her mother and daddy, to what they did and what they built. This is Opal Hunt's life, and she's so proud of it, she's inviting you in to see for yourself.

You can find her off FM 1086, she's about a 1/2 mile west on 83. It's a good idea to call before you go. 915-767-3183 (store) or 915-767-2188 (home)

114   *Enjoying a warm stove and good conversation with Opal Hunt.*

Dublin, Texas -
Pure Cane Goodness At
10, 2 and 4

One special thing about growing up in Texas in the 1950s was drinking Dr. Pepper. Folks up in New York never heard of "DP" until years later, but, in Texas, Dr. Pepper was a mainstay of beverages.

Stop #41
Dublin, TX

You could do all kinds of things with it, including drinking it hot with lemon, but the best way was to get one of the six ounce bottles right out of the machine and slam it down. My daddy always kept the temperature of the Dr. Pepper machine at his service station turned down to the point there was ice around the edges of the bottle when you popped the top. Whoo-boy that was good! Sometimes we'd pour in one of those nickel packages (60 cents today) of Spanish peanuts, and suddenly you'd have the perfect afternoon snack. Or morning snack. Whenever. Ten, two or four they said.

We still have Dr. Pepper of course, and it's still good stuff, but somewhere along the way they changed it. They may have even changed it for the better, I'm not sure, but as sure as I'm sitting here, they changed it. Dr. Pepper today does not taste exactly like the Dr. Pepper from my childhood.

What's the difference? Today they sweeten the stuff with corn syrup and such, but when I was a kid, pure cane sugar was what gave Dr. Pepper its pep.

Well guess what? Down in Dublin, Texas, they're still pouring 50 pound bags of Imperial Pure Cane into hundred gallon vats. Forget fake sugar, forget artificial sweeteners and forget your diet. This is the *real* real thing.

Bill Kloster, recently retired plant manager,

115

says they just don't do it like this any more. "We are the only plant in the world that still uses sugar," Bill says. "It costs a little more, but we feel like we are offering something special to the folks here in central Texas that grew up on this taste."

From the looks of it, you might not think this operation is too remarkable, unless you find it remarkable the machinery on the line runs at

Dr. Peppers bottled the old-fashioned way in Dublin.

all. The first time we were there the bottle washer broke down and since replacement parts disappeared during the last world war, some creative coaxing and bailing wire was in order. Minutes later, the Dublin Bottling Company was up and running, cranking out more DP from the oldest Dr. Pepper plant in the country. Over 100 years old.

In the office of the old plant you can still down a pepper for a dime. (Does anybody else out there remember when they raised the price from a nickel to six cents?)

Bill Kloster's first job here at the plant was here in the back of the building. The year was 1933, and Bill sorted bottles for 10 cents an hour. He ended up running the place. But there's even more history than that here, because this is the place where Dr. Pepper began. In 1891 S.H. Prim offered to take Wade Morrison's soda fountain concoction back to Dublin and put it in a bottle.

And now over 100 years later, it's Bill Kloster's grandson who climbs up to the mixing room once a week to prepare "the juice". Three hundred pounds of pure can sugar combined with a gallon of the magic syrup formula so secret that the recipe is kept in a bank vault in Dallas. A little fruit acid and some carbonated water, and another piece of bottled history trundles down the ancient assembly line.

The Dublin Bottling Company is located at 221 South Patrick in Dublin, off Highway 67 about a hundred miles southwest of Dallas. They are open from 9am-4:30pm weekdays with a break from 12 to 1 for lunch. Tours are free and we suggest that you call before you go out there so you can find out when they'll be bottling. 817-445-3466

"...We feel like we are offering something special to the folks here in central Texas..."
-Bill Kloster

The Magical Hot Wells Healing Waters

Stop #42
Young County, TX

"You can have a cut or a bruise and it will heal it...I can't explain it."
-a Stovall bather

We'd heard talk of a place folks were claiming was the fountain of youth. Yep, they said, there's a mineral bath near South Bend where hot water from the ground works like magic to cure what ails you. It seeps into your pores and tickles your innards. Regulars here say it will fix arthritis, rheumatism, stiff joints and aching backs. Some folks even claim it will cure the common cold. Of course we went to South Bend to find the magic. What we found was a place called Stovall Hot Wells, the last mineral bath house in the state. In a network of pipes and valves, the dark, oily water bubbles up from deep within the earth...natural heat, natural minerals, natural believers.

"You can have a cut or a bruise and it will heal it," one bather says. "I can't explain it. It's just a magical healing water or something."

The story of the Stovall Hot Wells began in 1929 when folks hoping to strike oil got water instead. The stuff was hot, about 130 degrees, and people were warned to stay away. But a few of the more daring folks jumped in for a swim...and soon they noticed an absence of aches and pains.

E.C. Stovall, who owned the land, accommodated people who wanted to take advantage of the water's healing powers by providing a tub and cabin for their use.

More and more people came and bath tubs were added. Soon bathers were declaring relief from rheumatism, athletes foot, eczema, kidney trouble, heat, ring worm, hay fever, poison ivy, colds, scalp diseases, stiff joints, soft gums, poor circulation and skin disorders.

For many years the Hot Wells enjoyed a booming business, but with the discovery of penicillin and the convenience of modern medicine the steady flow of patients dried up.

Today the Stovall Hot Wells are owned and operated by Dr. M.A. Strickland.

Whether it works or why it works, we don't know, yet the folks who come here leave

Hot Wells, the home of mineral baths and massages.

happy. The baths are open seven days a week, the water is maintained at a temperature of 101 degrees and you can even get a massage with your bath.

You can find the Stovall Hot Wells two miles northwest of South Bend in Young County, 10 miles southwest of Graham, on farm road 701 just past the Clear Fork River. The cost is just $6 for a bath (+ towel rental). They are open Monday through Saturday 9am to 6pm and Sunday 1pm to 5pm. 817-362-4423

Hotel Turkey...
A Museum With a Bed
You Can Sleep In

Stop #43
Turkey, TX

Out on the Panhandle caprock, between Lubbock and Amarillo, the wind is eroding eons of time, peeling back the layers to reveal a different moment in history. That same wind has blown through Turkey, Texas, changing the face of the place from boom town to bust and back again. That same wind has whistled past the front porch of Hotel Turkey.

Scott Johnson and his wife Jane left the good life in the city for an even better one way out in Turkey, Texas. Everyone thought they were crazy. When they went from Denton to Turkey, folks in Denton didn't understand. Folks in Turkey didn't even understand. But Scott and Jane knew exactly what they were doing. Scott's family reunions were held in Turkey every year, so he already knew the town. And he knew that if he didn't buy the hotel, he and his relatives might not have a place to stay.

Over the past few years, the Johnsons have worked hard to change the once dusty, dank hotel into more than just a place to stay. It's a museum, of sorts. It's been a labor of love, with Scott and Jane doing all the work themselves. Seven days a week, untold hours per day, but they say it's not a stressful job. Just the opposite, in fact. Whatever ails them, they say, can be cured with a good nights sleep...something you can get at the Hotel Turkey.

In the parlor you'll find an old phonograph from the 1920s. On it plays a 1920s era record. It's all part of setting the mood for the guests at the Hotel Turkey.

"You get to actually experience the 1920s," Jane explained. "Your food, the way we prepare it, the way it's cooked, even on the old stoves. Your linens for your bed are hung out on the clothesline to dry to give them that good fresh air feel and smell. That brings back memories of grandmother."

You won't find any rope chains and "do not touch" signs in this museum. Everything here

Innkeepers Scott and Jane Johnson in the Hotel Turkey parlor.

works and you're welcome to use it. In fact, this is the only museum in Texas where you can spend the night. You are encouraged to actively participate in your stay rather than just sit around. Lots of guests visit the kitchen and end up helping to cook the meals. It's not unusual for Jane to hand you some flour, a rolling pin and a recipe and ask you to make some old fashioned cookies...the kind grandma used to make. It's all part of the total experience of staying at the Hotel Turkey.

The museum showcases are, of course, the rooms. There you can sleep in grandma's feather bed. Everything you see is just like grandma saw, from the pictures on the wall to the curtains on the window. If you want to take a spin around town, Gobbler, the family horse, will gladly take you sightseeing in a buggy. And, for entertainment, forget HBO and Showtime. You won't even get Headline News here...don't need it. Our old friend Dennis Gaines, the cowboy poet, regularly recites in the parlor. The same parlor where Bob Wills, a Turkey native, got his start in western swing music.

"You get to actually experience the 1920s..."
-Jane Johnson

Scott and Jane say Hotel Turkey is actually their home...they just happen to have a lot of bedrooms. The folks who come to spend the night are actually their friends...they just haven't met them yet. They are more than a hotel, they're an experience.

Hotel Turkey sits at 3rd and Alexander in Turkey, Texas. They offer bed and breakfast, family and multiple day rates. There is tennis, fishing, a horse and buggy, and even a Llama. They were ranked #9 in Best Accomodations by Texas Highways in 1992. They also have area tours based out of the hotel that you don't want to miss. We advise you to call for reservations well in advance. 1-800-657-7110

A Shrine to Wire and the Road That Split the Prairie

Probably one of man's basic instincts is to delineate his property from other people's property, to claim his "stuff" so no one else will, to say "this is mine." The folks who settled Texas knew very well how to do this, and, if you've ever wondered what Texas looked like <u>before</u> the settlers, do this: find yourself a nice unplowed prairie and stare off into the distance while holding something across the bottom part of your field of vision. That's just about what it looked like. Everything you see now <u>except</u> the barbed wire fences.

Stop #44
McLean, TX

It was barbed wire that changed the face of Texas. Ranchers put it up to keep <u>their</u> cattle in <u>their</u> pasture. Farmers put it up to keep the ranchers' cattle, which previously roamed the open land, out of their fields. Pretty soon the state was cut up into pieces of "mine" and "theirs". What's interesting is that there wasn't just one kind of barbed wire. It came in all kinds of variations, from tame to darn near lethal. Some of the wire was treated with razor sharp points to make sure nobody tried to outsmart it. There were as many kinds of barbed wire as there were places to put it. The prickly, twisty metal was blessed and cursed. "Devil's rope" some called it.

Delbert True has spent most of his life in McLean, Texas, fascinated with barbed wire.

"Barbed wire is what made it possible to settle the west," he says. "It had a lot more to do with it than the six gun. A lot more of a cowboy's time is spent putting up and repairing barbed wire than any other thing he does."

There is one more thing that cut across the Texas Panhandle, and Delbert has a fascination with that, too. Route 66. The first road that really put America together allowed you to travel from Chicago to Santa Monica and see everything in between.

"We like to call it 'the mother road'," Delbert says. "Everybody kind of fled to the road hoping it would take them to better things and

Route 66, the famed highway that connected America together.

better times in their life."

Okay, so what do barbed wire and Route 66 have to do with one another, other than the fact that Delbert True is fascinated with them both? Well, that's it, really. Delbert is so fascinated with barbed wire and Route 66 that he operates The Barbed Wire and Route 66 Museum in McLean, Texas.

"People like to retrace their routes," Delbert says. "We have people come here who fled the dust bowl down Route 66 and they're trying to remember. We have people who grew up on some of these old ranches who recognize a particular spread by the type of barbed wire they used. We want to show how things used to be here in the Texas Panhandle. We want people who experienced it to remember how hard things were and we want people who weren't around then to know how hard things were for those before them."

The Barbed Wire and Route 66 Museum is located at 100 Kingsley Street in McLean, Texas. From April to November they are open 10am to 4pm Tuesday through Saturday and 1pm to 4pm on Sunday. In winter they are open on Fridays and Saturdays 10am to 4pm, Sunday 1pm to 4pm. Admission is free but donations are appreciated. They've had over 10,000 visitors, including the Smithsonian. 806-779-2225

"We want people who experienced it to remember how hard things were and we want people who weren't around then to know how hard things were for those before them."
-Delbert True

Cowboy Mornin':
Breakfast on the Ranch

Stop #45
Palo Duro Canyon, TX

"...we're not going to endure forever, but the canyon may."
-Tom Christian

Some folks say Palo Duro is Tom Christian's canyon. His grandfather settled here over a hundred years ago and his father ran cattle in the canyon's bottom. Tom was born in the same little house where his daddy was born. Three generations of the Christian family living and working on the edge of Palo Duro Canyon. Palo Duro Canyon is 120 miles long, 20 miles wide at places, and often more than 1100 feet deep, and nobody knows Palo Duro like Tom.

"Every mornin' when you start up and you look out over this canyon, you can't help but feel a certain amount of awe," Tom says. "It makes you realize just how limited the contribution can be...we're not going to endure forever, but the canyon may."

In these times of turbulent cattle prices, Tom Christian has found another way to keep his Figure 3 Ranch in the family. He's sharing his canyon. For those willing to get up before the chickens and make the trek out of Amarillo to the Christian spread near Claude, an experience unlike any other awaits. It's called "Cowboy Mornin'"and it's exactly what it says.

For a small fee, you can watch the dramatic painting on the land that occurs every morning in Palo Duro. Tom will even serve you breakfast, an old fashioned biscuits and gravy cowboy breakfast right out of the back of a real chuckwagon. Real cowboys, like Tom Christian, will pour you a cup of coffee in a tin cup. And you, too, can be in awe of Palo Duro Canyon.

Breakfast is $19 for adults, $14.50 for children over 3. Group rates are available. The Figure Three Ranch is 8 miles south of Claude on FM 1258. 1-800-658-2613

The Chevy Man

Unless you look close, you will probably miss it. Unless you are just in the habit of taking a notice to junk yards, Bill Clement's place will probably not catch your eye.

For all practical purposes that's exactly what Bill Clement has -- a junkyard. Here in Bill's yard you'll find hundreds of rusty, rotten reminders of automobiles past.

Stop #46
Lubbock, TX

But truth be known, this is more than just a junk yard. What Bill Clement *really* has is the self-proclaimed largest collection of old Chevrolets in the known universe. It's no wonder folks around here just call Bill, "The Chevy Man".

You probably will never find anyone, anywhere who knows more about old Chevy's than Bill. Over the years he's owned 4,000 of them. Some he's sold, some he's kept and some he's used for parts. Some are suitable for restoration and some have found their final resting place. Bill says ever car tells a story.

"Every one of them speak. They all grieve over the inhuman punishment they've received throughout their lives," he says.

As far as Bill is concerned, Chevrolet stopped making cars in 1972. That was the last year for the gas guzzling muscle cars, and Bill says it was the last year for the American love affair with the automobile.

"That's why spark plugs come eight to a box," Bill says with a laugh. "If you asked me, if it ain't got eight cylinders, it ain't a Chevrolet."

Whenever Bill gets the urge, he pulls one of his rusty old hulks into his garage and begins restoration. With the accumulation of parts from 4,000 Chevys, Bill can in effect make a new 1955 Bel Air convertible from ground up.

We walked through the final resting place for old Chevys with Bill while he told us the story behind some of them.

"This one isn't even good as dumpster bait," he says about one old station wagon. "It's got so much bondo on it, you can't even sell it as scrap metal cause there ain't much metal left. One more old, dead soldier."

Another sad example of what Bill calls a "sick item" appears to be an attempt to do a homemade conversion of a sedan to a pickup truck.

"Someone took a tomahawk to this poor old car," Bill says, "and they did know how to use a cutting torch."

But lots of Bill's cars are perfect for restoration. One 1956 Bel Air convertible looked like it had just come off the General Motors assembly line, "good as new"...at least we thought.

"They're never as good as new," Bill says, "cause nobody knows how to build cars like The General."

Still, they looked good to us. Ran great, too, when we took it for a spin through the cotton fields around Lubbock. Pictures Bill showed us of "before" were almost unbelievable. The car looked like one of those we frequently see parked behind someone's barn. Probably was, too. But when Bill Clement got through, well, you'll just have to go see for yourself. The price tag: $30,000, or about fifteen times the new price.

Bill Clement is located on Quirt Avenue (now called Martin Luther King Boulevard) in Lubbock. But here's the deal. Bill is a little different. He wants to be. And he doesn't like folks to just drop by. I'm not sure of their origin, but there are bullet holes in the front wall of his place that look like they came from inside, so ALWAYS call Bill before going to

"If you asked me, if it ain't got eight cylinders, it ain't a Chevrolet."
-Bill Clement

visit him. NEVER just stop by. It might not be healthy. Still, he'll be glad to show you his old Chevys and new Chevys if you will call at least a week in advance and make an appointment. Otherwise, you're on your own. 806-747-4848

Bill Clement puts the finishing touch on a 1955 Bel Air.

Dean Leonard's
Hand-Made Hats

Stop #47
Lubbock, TX

"This is hat country, and you can spot a good hat or a bad hat a mile away."
-Dean Leonard

There are men who are artists and craftsmen who are born into the business of making things -- sons and grandsons who are handed down a trade learned through years of apprenticeship. They are men who carry on a hand-made tradition of the American dream. Dean Leonard is *not* one of those men.

Dean was a farmer. He wasn't born into that business either, but for the last thirty-five years or so, Dean had spent his days, nights and most every weekend sweatin' his life away on top of a tractor. But when farming started going bad, Dean started looking for a way out. So one day just three years ago, Dean called it quits.

"It got to the point that you had to hock the farm just to start a crop," Dean says. "So I just quit. I walked away and decided to do something else."

What Dean did was find a friend that knew a thing or two about the hat business, bought some old antique equipment, hired a couple of part-time helpers and set up shop making hats. Today he's turning out custom-made hats as fast as you can tip your Stetson.

Now when Dean says "custom hand made hat" he means it. The only thing they do by machine here is sew a zig-zag stitch to attach the hat band.

Without doubt there is an art to hat making. It takes a keen eye and a knowing hand to get things just right. But for most of the folks who come in to Dean's shop, a hat is not an art object, or a fashion statement. Out on the south plains of Lubbock, a good hat is just a part of life.

"People out here wear hats to work, to

church, and every social function," Dean says with a smile. "This is hat country, and you can spot a good hat or a bad hat a mile away."

Now if you've ever bought a pair of custom boots, you know there's no feeling quite like slippin' on a pair that was made just for your feet. Well, a custom hat is the same way. It's a personal kind of thing.

If you know exactly what you want, Dean

Dean Leonard blocks one of his hand-made hats.

will take phone orders. In fact, he's had calls from all over the world. But if you really want a treat, stop in at Dean's shop and spend the best part of the day watching Dean cut, block and crease. He'll be happy to show you just what it takes to make a good hat.

You can find the Dean Leonard Hat Shop at 3215 34th Street in Lubbock, or you can give them a call at 806/791-0550. They are open Tuesday through Saturday 10am to 5:30pm. Be sure to tell Dean we said "Hello".

God's Country--
A South Plains Summer
Event

Stop #48
Crosbyton, TX

There's not a whole lot of anything in Crosby County, Texas, but cotton. Just take a look across the endless countryside and you'll see vast fields of neat rows that stretch all the way to the horizon. Crosbyton is the county seat. A town of 2,200, there's not much there, either, except of course for cotton and the farmers who make a living from it. For folks out here, cotton is a way of life.

Crosbyton does have what the locals say is the largest cotton gin in the world. We're not certain, but we can tell you it's really big.

For fifty weeks of the year, not much happens in Crosby County. Farmers get up early, tend to their fields, hit the sack after the local news and start over again the next morning.

But for two very special weeks in August, almost everyone in Crosby County heads for the Blanco Canyon Amphitheater to watch their history come to life.

It's called "God's Country", and folks from all around show up to watch friends and neighbors sing, dance and act out the history of the south plains. Sit back and enjoy a warm night of summer fun, and you just might learn something about Blanco Canyon and its wild west history.

Just about everybody in town gets involved, so, as you might expect, the "God's Country" musical is the biggest event of the year.

The local heritage foundation wrote the script, real farmers and real cowboys play the parts and sing the songs. The music is original too -- composed and arranged on the edge of Blanco Canyon by Rick Sudduth, who, by no surprise, is a cotton farmer.

"Somebody suggested we ought to have original music, so I just got to work on it." Rick says. "I never learned to read or write music, but if I can get a tune down on tape, somebody else can write it all out."

"I still live less than a mile from where I was born. To me this is God's Country," Rick tells us with a prideful smile.

In 1994, the people of Crosby county will perform "God's Country" for the ninth year.

The musical drama opens with Rick's "God's Country Theme" and rolls along for the next two hours with a dozen or so tunes that will have your toes tapping and your hands clapping all the while telling the story of the settling of the plains.

To get to the Blanco Canyon Amphitheater, take US 82 east out of Lubbock to Crosbyton then take FM 651 north for 10 and a half miles and follow the signs to the Amphitheater.

"God's Country" runs in early August each year for two weeks. The amphitheater seats 700 and tickets can be ordered in advance. They are $7 per person. For more information and ticket reservations call 806/675-2331.

"I still live less than a mile from where I was born. To me this is God's Country..."
-Rick Sudduth

Black Vinyl Memories at The Big Spring Record Shop

Stop #49
Big Spring, TX

"Elvis used to drop by here when he was peddling records for the old Sun label...Dad told him he wouldn't make it unless he changed his sound."

-Jake Glickman

Jake Glickman's dad never threw anything away. He was a pack rat. In the 1930s he owned juke boxes which were filled with records. No matter how bad the recording or how obscure the artist, he never threw them out. He kept them. For years and years he kept them. He had a bad habit of overbuying for his juke boxes and couldn't bear to send back the extras, thus, vintage virgin vinyl.

Jake Glickman is following in his dad's groove. He too has kept all those recordings which never got thrown away and still offers them for sale at The Record Shop in Big Spring, Texas. Today Jake Glickman has one of the largest collection of unplayed records in the world. At The Record Shop you can find new Richie Valens and never played Herman's Hermits. They have a new copy of "A Touch of Today" by Nancy Wilson and "Early Hits of 1964" by Lawrence Welk. If you like old music, and you want to buy it in mint condition, The Record Shop has everything from rock and roll, big band, jazz, pop, country and western, records which probably can't be found in more than two or three places in the country. You'll find a copy of "Sing Along Banjo Party" and "ABC" by the Jackson Five. There's Jimi Hendrix's "Moods" and just about everything ever done by Black Sabbath. And, if you like music history, this place was visited by "The King".

"Elvis used to drop by here when he was peddling records for the old Sun label," Jake explained. "Dad told him he wouldn't make it unless he changed his sound. He stopped by several times and Dad always gave him advice about his music, telling him he didn't think anybody would buy the stuff but he'd carry it anyway."

What you see on the floor at The Record Shop just scratches the surface. Jake Glickman keeps most of his 130,000 records in an underground vault. The real treasures are located there and can only be retrieved by Jake. Don't see what you want? Just ask. The popular and the obscure are found there. In 1974, Evel Knievel recorded an album that no one bought. No one except The Record Shop, that is, and you'll find several copies there...if, for any reason, you should want one. You can find 45s and 78s. If it was recorded on vinyl, chances are you can find it at The Record Shop.

The Record Shop is located at 211 Main Street in Big Spring. They are open from 10am to 5:30pm Monday through Saturday. They are closed on Sundays. 915-267-7501

Jake Glickman among the thousands of albums at The Record Shop. 135

Strange Goings Ons in the West Texas Desert

Stop #50
Marfa, TX

Probably one of the most often asked questions is "Bob, where do you get your story ideas?" Everywhere we go people inquire about the origin of the tales we tell every week. Fact is, we get our story ideas from all kinds of sources...small town newspapers (if you haven't read a good Texas weekly from a town of 5,000 or so, you're missing out; stuck in between the obits and the feed store ads you'll find some great human interest features), letters, phone calls, folks even stop us on the road to tell us about "a guy I know who...". Point is, our story ideas come from anywhere we can get them. I guess the only trick is being able to distinguish between the ones nobody wants to hear and the ones everybody wants to hear. Sometimes we're successful in that, sometimes we're not.

Then, too, there's the "different factor". See, we figure everybody has heard about the Willie Nelsons of Texas but few have heard about Milton Watts so we do stories about Miltons and rarely about Willies. If they're already famous you probably won't see them on our show. If you've heard of them before, they're probably too famous for us. In other words, we look for the "unheard of".

For every rule there's an exception. Ours is called the "Marfa Lights." Just about everybody in Texas has heard of the Marfa Lights. It's an old story that goes back at least as far as cowboy and Indian days, though we've heard tales that the "Lights" have been around Marfa since the days of Spanish explorers, maybe longer. And even though its an old story that just about everyone has heard, we traveled to Marfa to do a story on the famous Marfa Lights.

Just in case you're one of the few who never heard tale of the Marfa Lights, we'd like to tell you what they are. We'd like to, but we can't. Nobody can. Oh, there are plenty of theories, but no one knows <u>for sure</u>. The only thing we <u>can</u> tell you is that some folks say there's something out there on the desert south of Marfa.Few folks in the adobe and whitewashed town agree on what they are or even <u>if</u> they are.

The night we visited Marfa to look for the lights folks were lined up at a favorite viewing spot next to the highway. It's like that just about every evening, with people from all over the world stopping to see if the story is true. Did we see them? Yes. Well, maybe. Depends on what "they" are, and, like we said, we're not really sure.

There are stories of Marfa Lights sightings from the times when cowboys drove cattle across the Mitchell Flat, but certainly the story became more popular during World War II. The U.S. Army operated an air base near Marfa in those days, and there were lots of reports of strange lights seen by pilots. Electricity had not yet made its way to the farms and ranches in the area, but airmen like Fritz Kahl swore there was something out there.

"We could see the lights on the horizon when we were taking off and landing from the air strip, but when you flew over the spot where you thought they originated, there was nothing there," he says.

Researchers will tell you that most of what people claim to see across the desert is actually headlights from cars, but that would require some pretty convoluted refraction since there is

"We could see the lights on the horizon when we were taking off and landing from the air strip, but when you flew over the spot where you thought they originated, there was nothing there."
-Fritz Kahl

only one road and it is clearly visible. The lights do not always originate from the area of that road, and, if they did, one scientist estimated that any car would have to be traveling several hundred miles an hour to match the speed of the Marfa Lights.

So, what are they? We don't know, but it makes for a great evening, if you're interested in taking a look for yourself.

To see the Marfa Lights, go southeast on Hwy 190 from Marfa and pull over at one of the parking lots you'll see on the right hand side of the road. The best time to go is on clear evenings just after sundown.

By the way, when you get to the Big Bend area, you'll only be able to pick up one radio station. It's KVLF, 1240 on the AM dial, the "VLF" part stands for "voice of the last frontier", which this area of Texas truly is. When you travel from an area where stations are crammed together on the dial, it's kind of neat to have only one choice.

Ray Hendrix hosts the morning show. If you give him a call, he just might play you a tune.

The Rock Ranch...
If You Can't Sell Cattle,
Sell Rocks

The hills and valleys of the Davis Mountains in far west Texas have been home to cattle ranching for so long, nobody can remember which came first: the cowboy or the cactus. Together they've stubbornly stuck to the landscape that paints this rocky, rugged country. Fifty years ago out here cattle prices were as jumpy as jackrabbits in a prairie fire. Back then, Frank Woodward realized it would take more than beef to keep the family ranch, it would darn near take a miracle...like all the worthless rocks that dot his place turning into gold.

That's when Frank found paydirt. The rocks he'd tripped over and cursed all his life were the secret to survival. In no time, they were calling Frank's place "The Rock Ranch."

They call them agates, stones exploding with plumes of fiery complexion. Born in volcanic lava 43 million years ago, the agate plumes lay like hidden treasure inside otherwise ordinary looking stone. Cut and polished, they erupt into a kaleidoscope of color. If you just look at them, they're beautiful. Most folks think the rocks have a fern trapped inside.

Fifty years after her grandfather spread the word about Woodward Rock Ranch, Susan Woodward is still raising rocks right along with the cattle. Over the years, the agates and opals of the Woodward Ranch have lured rock hounds from around the world. They are free to roam 4,000 acres, picking up stones for pennies a pound.

At the Woodward Ranch, novices and experts alike browse a veritable library of lapidation.

Stop #51
Alpine, TX

"I think when times are tough and you're trying to live off the land, anything you can do to keep the ranch in the family is pretty serious."
-Susan Woodward

Susan helps choose the chunks hiding millions of years of treasure. For the novice, the most exciting part is finding something that looks like a piece of rock, having Susan cut it open and discovering something amazing inside.

For all their fire and beauty, their interest and appeal, the rocks of the Woodward Ranch are neither diamonds nor gold. Life out here is still as rough and rugged as the landscape Frank Woodward rode over half a century ago. All around her, Susan has seen the neighbor ranches steadily sell out to weekend cowboys riding high on big city bank rolls. Like her grandfather before her, Susan continues to live off the land and struggles to keep the land in the family.

"Ever since I was a little girl, my father has told us that when we grew up we could come back here," Susan says. "When you are in a position like I'm in now, you realize that you don't ever own the land, the land owns you."

You can be a part of the survival of a family ranch and pick up some pretty neat rocks at the same time. The Woodward Rock Ranch is 16 miles south of Alpine on Highway 118. They are down an all weather county road. You'll see the sign. It's $3 a day if you just want to hike around the area, and 50 cents a pound for the agates you want to take with you. Primitive campsites and RV hookups are also available. They are open 8am until dark everyday. They do ask that you call before you come out. 915-364-2271

The Loneliest Library
In Texas

There is great controversy about the most unique area of Texas. Some say it is paradise. Others claim it looks like the surface of the moon. Welcome to Big Bend.

Big Bend is Texas as we saw it in old westerns on television and Saturday mornings at the movies. It is a Hollywood backlot come to life and dropped in an unlikely corner of the state southeast of El Paso, just across the border from Mexico and half a million miles away from the concrete and glass of places like Houston and Dallas. Or, so it seems. Big Bend is a world of its own.

Smack dab in the middle of Big Bend is a tiny one burro town called Redford. It is farther from Redford to a commercial airport than any other town in the lower 48 states. One look around and you have to ask yourself what you're doing here. True, Redford is no garden spot. Fact is, there is little reason for anyone to come here, even fewer reasons for those already here to stay. One writer said of this place, "I felt as if I had come to the last path of the earth."

The kids growing up in Redford don't have any theaters...or fast food restaurants...or shopping malls to hang out in. There are no electronic games or parks nearby. They didn't even have a library...until Lucia Madrid decided there are some things a kid just can't do without. When Lucia was growing up here she didn't have a single book to call her own. By the time she came back here to teach, she figured things had changed. They had not.

"My father came to live here," Lucia says in her thick Spanish accent. "My mother was

Stop #52
Redford, TX

born here and I was born here, too. When I first came to school, for the first three years I didn't have a book. And I love books. Now I have more books than I can read."

Welcome to Lucia Madrid's Library. It's probably not at all like any library you've ever seen. Lucia's library is located in a corner of her grocery store on the only street through Redford. Actually, these days it's the grocery

Lucia Madrid in her library with a young reader.

store that fights for space. The books are crowding the place, and that suits Lucia just fine.

Lucia started gathering books and magazines, encyclopedias and catalogs anywhere she could get them. Sears catalogs, she discovered, made excellent dictionaries because they had pictures and words together...and they were easy to come by. In no time at all, Lucia needed shelves. A milkman who made a stop at the grocery store supplied blue milk crates, most of which are still being used in Lucia's Library today. Hardly the stuff of big city libraries, but Lucia thinks they're beautiful. On a wall near the cash register is the Lucia's Library Hall of Fame -- Redford kids who have gone on to make it -- an engineer, doctors, teachers. Pictures proudly displayed here as a challenge to those who come after them.

"I had a little girl in the Head Start program," Lucia says. "Now she is an industrial engineer in Midland. Hundreds of kids have gone on to be teachers and doctors and lawyers. They couldn't have done it without books."

There is one thing bad about Lucia's Library. After reading the books, she says, the children leave Redford...and rarely return. That's okay, she says. There will be other children.

To get to Redford, Texas, take 67 south from Marfa to Presidio, then 170 south to Redford. The Madrid Store is on your left and the library is just inside. Stop by and read a book. Better yet, fill the trunk of your car before you make the trip and leave some books behind. You'll be making a contribution to our future. The library is open in the afternoons, but call first to make sure Lucia is there. 915-384-2339

"When I first came to school, for the first three years I didn't have a book. And I love books. Now I have more books than I can read."
-Lucia Madrid

TRAVEL NOTES